WWII
CODEBREAKERS
AND SPIES

ANDRE
DEUTSCH

CONTENTS

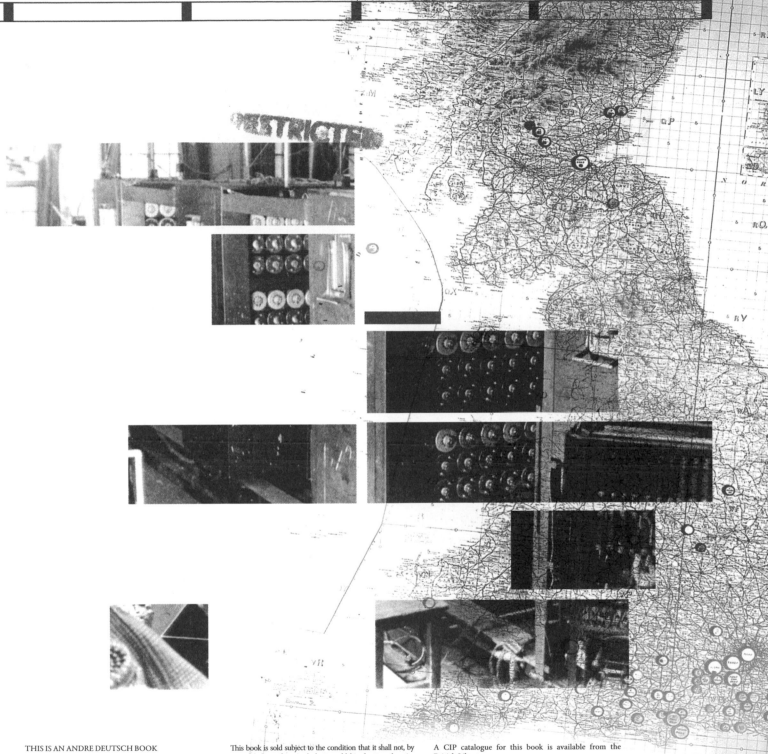

THIS IS AN ANDRE DEUTSCH BOOK

Design © Andre Deutsch 2019
Text copyright © Michael Smith 2011

First published in 2011 under the title *Britain's Secret War*.
This edition published in 2019 by Andre Deutsch
20 Mortimer Street
London
W1T 3JW

A CIP catalogue for this book is available from the
British Library.
ISBN: 978 0 233 00602 4

Front cover photographs: The National Archives, UK
& (bottom right) Author collection
Back cover photograph: (top) Bletchley Park Trust &
(bottom) Private Collection
Spine photograph: SSPL/Getty Images

INTRODUCTION

The success enjoyed by Britain's spies during the Second World War stands in stark contrast to the popular perception of bungling spooks that emerged during the post-war period, when Britain's intelligence services appeared incapable of preventing the Soviet Union's KGB from placing spies at every level of the British establishment, with the Cambridge spy ring even succeeding in infiltrating the highest echelons of MI5 and MI6 themselves.

A t the start of the twenty-first century, the failures of the intelligence services over the existence of Iraqi weapons of mass destruction and the 7/7 al-Qaeda bombings in London appeared to follow a similarly depressing pattern. By contrast, the brilliance displayed by Britain's codebreakers in cracking the German Enigma cipher, and the stunning successes of the Double Cross system in deceiving the German spymasters who sent their agents into the United Kingdom, seem unrepeatable masterstrokes. This perception is almost certainly misleading. By their very nature, intelligence failures inevitably become public, while successes usually result in nothing going wrong and remain untrumpeted. We do not know how often MI5, MI6 and the latter-day codebreakers at GCHQ have saved British lives, silently (as is the way with any good spy). But as more and more of the records of Britain's Second World War intelligence services are released to the National Archives, new and previously untold successes have emerged, making it clear that, whatever the truth about today's spies, their predecessors played a vital part in winning the war. The extraordinary story of the collection of eccentric intellectuals who worked at Bletchley Park breaking a variety of enemy codes and ciphers throughout the war has been public knowledge since the mid-1970s, but even now new detail is emerging and new generations learn with astonishment, and not a little national pride, of their remarkable successes. Stirring biographies of the heroes and villains who inhabited the world of the Secret War reveal new details of men like the double agent Eddie Chapman, a crook and womanizer, whose codename ZigZag accurately reflected the ambiguity of his own personality, or of thrilling operations to con the Germans into placing their defences in the wrong places, allowing the allies to get ashore in Normandy and Sicily during the invasion of occupied Europe, and thereby saving countless lives. But there were failures as well as successes. Many brave men and women died during the Secret War. This book is designed to guide you through both the failures and successes, and to give you a feel of who the people involved in them were and what they did.

So what were the organizations that took part in Britain's Secret War? The most famous British intelligence service is that which we now know as MI6, the real title of which is the Secret Intelligence Service (SIS), the organization that collects intelligence overseas. It embraces the archetypal human spies who have appeared in the classic espionage stories, like John le Carré's George Smiley and Ian Fleming's James Bond, a hero based on Fleming's own experience during the Secret War, when his job as a naval intelligence officer was to liaise between the Admiralty and SIS. The use of the alternative title MI6 began during the Second World War in an attempt to make it sound as if it was just another section of military intelligence: MI6 was the military intelligence section that liaised with SIS. There is a continuing, erroneous belief that MI6 was a complete failure during the Second World War, but new detail from the documents released to the National Archives shows this to be yet another false perception.

The domestic intelligence agency is the Security Service, MI5, which is responsible for tracking down foreign spies operating in the United Kingdom, as well as what we now call terrorists – although during the Secret War these would have been German sabotage agents attempting to damage the war effort. It started the war in a very poor state, but swiftly became extremely efficient at tracking down German spies, and took the lead in the Double Cross system, turning them against their Nazi spymasters to feed false information back to Berlin.

The real name of the codebreaking organization commonly known as Bletchley Park was the Government Code and Cypher School (GC&CS), which had been set up in the immediate aftermath of the First World War. It was an amalgamation of the wartime military codebreaking organization MI1b and its much better known, and more successful, naval counterpart, which was known as Room 40 from the offices in the Admiralty in which it worked. Its public role was ensuring the codes and ciphers used by various government departments and the armed forces were accurate. Its secret role was breaking the codes and ciphers of other countries, whether or not they were Britain's enemies. At one point in the immediate aftermath of the First World War, the United States was one of the codebreakers' top targets and it remained an important priority right up to America's entry into the Second World War following the Pearl Harbor attack of December 1941. GC&CS was controlled throughout the war by the head of MI6.

The fourth of the main agencies involved in fighting the Secret War was the Special Operations Executive, the SOE, which began as a couple of small sections within MI6 and the War Office working to carry out sabotage behind enemy lines, but was elevated by Churchill to become one of the most important components of the Secret War. Churchill told SOE's bosses to "set Europe ablaze", by placing agents on the ground inside the countries occupied by the Germans to carry out sabotage and assassination missions and to give active support to local resistance organizations.

Although these were the four main agencies within the Secret War, there were a number of others. All three of the armed forces had their own intelligence departments which were highly critical of MI6. The Naval Intelligence Division even considered setting up its own secret service but its head, Admiral John Godfrey, was dissuaded from doing so by Ian Fleming, then the naval intelligence officer in charge of liaising with MI6. The Military Intelligence Directorate included MI9, which ran escape lines for British forces trapped in enemy territory, some of whom had escaped from Prisoner-of-War (PoW) camps, while others were separated from their units during fighting or were RAF aircrew who had been shot down. MI9 had the additional role of collecting intelligence, both from PoWs, mainly by the use of letters written in code or secret ink and by debriefing the escapees on their return to the United Kingdom. The fact that it was collecting intelligence on the ground inside occupied territory meant that, while it was in theory part of the military intelligence apparatus, it was taken under the control of MI6. The final part of the Secret War was MI19 which interrogated German prisoners of war and used stool pigeons to encourage them to discuss secret information among themselves in conversations bugged by hidden microphones.

MICHAEL SMITH

MI6: WHAT IT WAS AND WHERE IT STARTED FROM

The Secret Intelligence Service, SIS, now better known as MI6, was set up in 1909 as a small section of a Secret Service Bureau, created primarily to track German spies who were wrongly assumed to be present all over the United Kingdom collecting intelligence ahead of the First World War.

LEFT Valentine Vivian, deputy to Menzies and head of Section V, the MI6 counter-espionage branch.

OPPOSITE LEFT Mansfield Cumming, founder and first chief of the British Secret Service.

OPPOSITE RIGHT Stewart Menzies, the chief of MI6 for most of the Second World War.

The bureau was split into a domestic section, which was headed by an army officer, Captain Vernon Kell, and a foreign section headed by a naval officer, Commander Mansfield Cumming. These divisions represented the respective interests of the two services, with the foreign section very much the junior partner. Its role was to act as a "screen" to liaise with spies, who might collect useful intelligence on Germany but were regarded as the type of person that no government official should be dealing with.

Cumming proved to be an excellent "chief" of the SIS, collecting a great deal of intelligence from agents operating inside Germany and later in Bolshevik Russia, where spies like Sidney Reilly and the author Arthur Ransome were much more useful than their romantic images suggest. He was responsible for three service traditions that exist to this day: the first being that the chief of the secret service is known as "C", which was originally derived from the first letter of Cumming's surname but subsequently stood for "chief"; that all reports should be sent out in red-coloured files with the prefix CX at the start of the reference number; and that C's letters should be written in green ink. Cumming was succeeded in 1923 by another naval

HUGH SINCLAIR (1873–1939)

Hugh Sinclair took over from Mansfield Cumming, the first head of MI6, when Cumming died in June 1923. Sinclair had a sizeable family fortune and was fond of good living, earning the nickname "Quex" after the lead character in a popular play, *The Gay Lord Quex*, who was described as "the wickedest man in London". But he made a sizeable contribution to the intelligence organizations which would fight the Secret War, setting up both the codebreaking Government Code and Cypher School, now better known as Bletchley Park, and Section D, which formed the basis for the Special Operations Executive. He also fought hard to ensure that MI6 had sufficient funds to produce vital intelligence on the German war effort.

officer, Admiral Hugh Sinclair, who was still in charge at the start of the Second World War.

Sinclair's officers in the major capitals abroad were usually hidden behind the cover of Passport Control Officer, based in the British embassy or consulate. In theory, they only ran agents into neighbouring countries (not into the one where they were actually stationed), although this rule was understandably ignored in Nazi Germany during the late 1930s. The service's headquarters was at Broadway Buildings in St James's, London, with operations on the ground controlled by "G" sections covering various geographical areas abroad and material passed on to the Circulating sections. The main sections were: Section I – Political, dealing largely with the Foreign Office; Section II – Air, dealing with the Air Ministry; Section III – Naval, working for the Admiralty; Section IV – Army, reporting to the War Office; Section V – Counter-Espionage and liaison with MI5; and Section VI – Economic Intelligence. Coverage of Germany was much better than is commonly believed, with exceptionally good intelligence available on German rearmament, which preceded Hitler's accession to power in 1933, but this was ignored by the British government until it was too late. The main problem for Sinclair was a dire lack of funds, and the refusal of British ambassadors in Japan and Switzerland (from where intelligence on Italy was collected) to allow secret service officers to operate from their embassies, which severely limited the availability of intelligence on both Japan and Italy. The gaps in intelligence on Italian intentions during the Abyssinia Crisis in 1935 forced Sinclair to write a forthright memo denouncing the paltry funding. The service's annual budget was by then £180,000, a level which had forced Sinclair to drop coverage of a number of countries completely. "Living, as it does, a hand to mouth existence, with vast areas to cover, it is, as things are, only possible for SIS to scratch the surface," he said. "To obtain really inside information means spending big money."

Sinclair demanded an extra million pounds a year; he got an increase to £350,000 a year. The extra funding allowed limited preparations for war. These included the creation of the Z organization, a network of journalists and businessmen operating across Western Europe under the control of Colonel Claude Dansey, a long-serving senior SIS officer. Dansey was ostensibly sacked for a financial fraud, but in fact continued working for Sinclair, running a parallel network of intelligence officers

LEFT Italian troops marching into Adigrat, one of the first towns to surrender to invading troops. MI6 set up a special operations unit called Section D (the D standing for Destruction) which operated behind Italian lines in Abyssinia.

OPPOSITE MI6 set up an air reconnaissance section under the Australian pilot Sidney Cotton which flew over Europe taking photographs of German bases and was eventually taken over by the RAF.

operating under civilian cover across Europe, independently of the Passport Control Officers, whose intelligence role was known to the governments of the countries in which they were based. Dansey used a number of front companies, including the export agency Geoffrey Duveen and Company, based at Bush House in the Aldwych in central London.

Sinclair also set up three new sections. One of them, Section VII, was to recruit "stay-behind" agents around the United Kingdom who would form an intelligence network in the event of a successful German invasion. Section VIII, under Richard Gambier-Parry, a former sales manager for the Philco wireless company, was to provide radio communications links between the United Kingdom and officers operating abroad, and to develop wireless transmitters to be used by agents operating behind enemy lines. The third, Section IX, was to carry out sabotage to hamper German and Italian war efforts. It swiftly became known as Section D, the "D" standing for Destruction. Lieutenant-Colonel Lawrence Grand, the Royal Engineer officer recruited by Sinclair to run the section, recalled being told that "nothing at all" was banned. "I was given an office on the ground floor with a bare table and chair and found next door another new boy, Gambier-Parry, who turned out to be a wireless expert," Grand said. "We were both very vague as to what we had to do, in fact, we soon realized that we had come to fill a complete vacuum. There were no real secret communications and there was no organization for anything except the collection of intelligence. We were starting from scratch with a vengeance." Sinclair also set up a photographic reconnaissance section under Frederick Winterbotham, the head of the air section, which employed an Australian pilot, Sidney Cotton, to fly over large areas of Europe and northern Africa photographing German and Italian military installations

to provide intelligence on what was going on and details of potential targets for RAF bombers.

Shortly after the war began, the Z organization's representative in Holland, Sigismund Payne-Best, and Major Richard Stevens, the Passport Control Officer in The Hague, were lured to a small hotel near Venlo on the Dutch–German border for a series of negotiations with opposition "emissaries" offering to depose Hitler. The emissaries were in fact members of the Sicherheitsdienst, the Nazi party's internal intelligence organization, and in what became known as "the Venlo Incident", Payne-Best and Stevens were kidnapped and taken to Berlin, giving the Nazis a major propaganda victory. The Z organization was blown, while the German advances across Europe deprived SIS of many of its agent networks.

CX REPORTS

MI6 reports are now routinely known as CX reports after the service's practice of preceding the serial numbers with CX. This bigram had been traditionally used within the Foreign Office for Confidential Exchange and dated back at least to the mid-nineteenth century, but it was adapted by Mansfield Cumming, the first "chief" of MI6, who apparently told an agent in Brussels: "If you have urgent material you want to get to us quickly you should put CX CX CX CX on the report" – denoting that it was for C and urgent. CX reports come in so-called "red" files, which are in fact buff files with a series of horizontal red lines across the top.

RIGHT Front page of the *Daily Mail* reports on the kidnap of SIS agents Richard Stevens and Sigismund Payne-Best during the Venlo Incident.

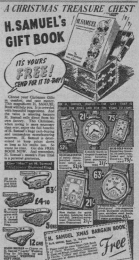

COPY FOR C.A.S.

MOST SECRET.

Separate copies sent to:-   C.A.S.

V.C.A.S.

A.C.A.S.(I).

OPERATIONS CARRIED OUT BY R.A.F. ON BEHALF OF S.I.S.

1.   I attach a table giving details of operations carried out by the R.A.F. for S.I.S. to date.

2.   After the defeat of France in June 1940, S.I.S. contacts with the Continent, which depended largely on communications through France, were wrecked. Agents in enemy countries, particularly in Italy, lost their means of communication. At the same time, the whole of Northern France became a theatre for S.I.S. operations, and demands for information from all sides were steadily increasing. Thus, S.I.S. was faced with additional and more difficult tasks, but was without the means of communication required to carry them out.

3.   Attempts to transport agents by sea were not entirely successful, owing to the vigilance of the Germans on the beaches. In August 1940, an attempt was made to land an agent by Lysander. S.I.S. were not experienced in that type of operation at the time, and this first essay was a failure. What happened is not known, as the aircraft did not return, and although the agent had a wireless set, nothing more was heard of him.

4.   By October 1940, more had been learnt, and two very successful operations were carried out during that month, thanks to the R.A.F. In the first of these, the organising agent was put back in a Lysander. Later he was picked up again. The organisation which resulted from this operation bore good fruits, and continued to provide good operational information until 1942. This included many reports on the movements of German battle-ships and their whereabouts in Western ports. In the second operation, a group of agents with wireless sets were dropped by parachute. This group constituted a most useful source of information until the middle of 1941, when the Germans arrested the head of the organisation and his wireless operator.

5.   Successful operations, including the picking up of agents, were carried out in March, April and May, 1941. It shoudl be noted that a picking-up operation is the best and quickest means of bringing back to this country not only agents who can then make detailed reports, but also masses of documents which would never pass the various frontiers if they were sent out through Lisbon.

6.   The picking up and dropping of agents and their wireless sets and operators continued throughout 1941, whenever the weather permitted. These operations proved to be invaluable.

./.   As an instance...

As an instance, I may quote the organisation set up by an agent whom I will call "X". This man was orginally put over by sea towards the end of 1940. He has built up an extensive organisation, which covers a very considerable area in Occupied France. Without the aid of the R.A.F., which enabled "X's" increasing demands for wireless operators, material, and other resources to be met, this organisation would have been of little value. This service gave the first news of the arrival of the German cruisers in the Brest area, and continued to supply most accurate reports of their whereabouts and the damage they had sustained, right up to the day before their break through the English Channel.

7.   In March 1942, the R.A.F. brought back "X", and with him a collection of maps and documents of over 100 lbs. in weight. The R.A.F. put him back again after he had been taught a new method of communication. From this operation in particular, we expect to derive useful operational information, and to get it more quickly than in the past.

8.   The difficulty of operating agents in this war appears to be greater than it was in the last, owing to the lack of neutral countries which adjoin enemy territory, and to which we can obtain easy access. Nevertheless, a large amount of air information is received from agents, although this may not be fully realised, because when this information is referred to in Air Intelligence reports and summaries, the source from which it came is seldom quoted.

9.   Agents have been particularly useful in reporting the movements of German naval vessels, and experience has shown that reports received from agents in the West coast of France and Norway regarding ship movements, have been accurate and fully confirmed by subsequent P.R.U. reconnaissance. Comparatively heavy losses in P.R.U. aircraft and trained pilots might have been considerably reduced if it had been found possible to place more reliance on agents' reports on ship movements, and hence to reduce the number of sorties sent over heavily defended areas.

10.   This Minute, and the attached table, are intended merely for your personal information. I hope in future to be able to keep you more closely informed of the co-operation between the R.A.F. and S.I.S., and of the results that have been thereby achieved. I also hope to be in a position to supply you with any detailed information on this subject which you may from time to time require.

D. of I. (L).
14.4.42.

Air Commodore.

S.I.S. AIR TRANSPORT OPERATIONS.

L Period.	Number scheduled.	Postponed or cancelled by "C".	Postponed or cancelled owing to weather or aircraft shortage.	Unsuccessfully attempted.	Successful operations.
October 1940 to end of August 1941.					18.
September 1941.	7	Nil	Nil	Nil	7.
October 1941.	11	3	Nil	Nil	8.
November 1941.	9	4	1	Nil	4.
December 1941.	7	2	1	1	3.
January 1942.	12	4	6	1	1.
February 1942.	14	3	8	2	1.
February/March 1942.	20	9	5	Nil	6.
March/April 1942.	10	1	1	Nil	8.
Totals, September 1941 to March 1942.	90	26	22	4	38.

These operations involved:-

(i)   The transport of 57 agents overseas.
(ii)   The return to U.K. of 18 agents.
(iii)   Five sorties for the dropping of material only.
(iv)   The loss of three aircraft (two Lysanders and one Whitley), of which the pilot of one Lysander was subsequently recovered.

THE CODEBREAKERS OF BLETCHLEY PARK

The breaking of the Enigma ciphers of the Wehrmacht (the German armed forces) at Bletchley Park is now widely recognized as a vital part of the Secret War.

LEFT Dilly Knox, the brilliant codebreaker whose career spanned both world wars and who broke the Abwehr Enigma.

OPPOSITE Bletchley Park Control, which co-ordinated interception of the main German radio links to ensure that the most important were always covered.

Britain's wartime codebreaking organization, the Government Code and Cypher School (GC&CS), had grown out of the success of the British Army and Royal Navy codebreaking sections during the First World War, particularly the work of Room 40, the naval codebreakers, who broke the Zimmerman Telegram, an enciphered message between Berlin and the German ambassador in Mexico that was used by Britain to bring the United States into the war, ensuring Germany's defeat.

In the early 1920s, GC&CS was brought under the control of Admiral Hugh Sinclair, the Chief of the Secret Intelligence Service, and spent much of the inter-war period working on Soviet codes and ciphers. German ciphers were largely ignored on the assumption that, since the Germans knew all about Room 40's success, their new ciphers, which used the Enigma cipher machine, would be bound to be "invincible".

During the late 1930s, increased attention was given to the Wehrmacht's ciphers, with Dilly Knox, a veteran of Room 40 and arguably one of the greatest of the British codebreakers, breaking the Enigma ciphers given by the Germans to their Spanish Republican allies during the Spanish Civil War. The British efforts to break the Enigma ciphers were hampered by modifications to the machine made by the Wehrmacht. But in 1939, French intelligence set up a series of meetings between Knox and Polish codebreakers, who, assisted by key settings provided by a French agent inside the German War Ministry,

had already broken the early German army Enigma machine ciphers. Knox was initially sceptical of the Polish success, but soon warmed to the young Polish mathematicians led by Marian Rejewski. Although the Polish codebreakers were struggling to cope with increased German security measures, the methods they used were to be the basis for the work of the British codebreakers, who adapted them and introduced their own improved techniques to keep up with the numerous new machine ciphers that emerged during the Second World War.

Like most of the Room 40 codebreakers, Knox was a classicist, and while his methods were highly effective, Alastair Denniston, the director of GC&CS, realized that mathematicians would have the right kind of brain to work out how to break the various different machine ciphers the codebreakers were now coming up against. He brought in Alan Turing and Peter Twinn, two leading mathematicians, to work on the Enigma material, and trawled the universities, signing up leading mathematicians to join GC&CS on the outbreak of war.

As part of his preparations for war, and in anticipation of heavy German bombing of London, Sinclair had bought a

ABOVE Bletchley Park, bought by Admiral Hugh Sinclair, the head of MI6, as the war station for all his staff but which became the home of the wartime codebreakers.

country estate at Bletchley to serve as a "war station" for both SIS and GC&CS. The codebreakers first moved to Bletchley Park during the Munich Crisis of September 1938 together with a number of MI6 sections for "a rehearsal". Sinclair put a Captain William Ridley RN, one of the MI6 officers, in charge of the operation. "MI6 provided some cars for transport, but many people used their own cars and gave lifts to others," Josh Cooper, head of Bletchley Park's air section, said. "It fell to my lot to be driven in by Knox who had a remarkable theory that the best way to avoid accidents was to take every cross-road at maximum speed." Shortly after they arrived at Bletchley, Neville Chamberlain returned from his talks with Hitler proclaiming "peace in our time", Cooper recalled. "We all trooped back to London with mixed feelings of shame and relief."

The codebreakers returned to Bletchley Park on 15 August 1939, more than two weeks before war broke out, and initially it seemed like they might have to go back to London yet again.

"The news in the papers was grave enough but there was still nothing in our material to indicate that Germany was on the brink of war," Cooper recalled. "Early in the morning of the 1st of September 1939, I met the admiral's deputy, Colonel Menzies, over breakfast in the old dining room in the house. I must have made some fatuous remark about another quiet night, to which he replied tersely: 'Heavy fighting all along the Polish frontier.'"

It was very soon clear that there would be insufficient room in the mansion to house all the people, many of them distinguished academics, who were now arriving to work at Bletchley Park (they were by no means all mathematicians and had originally included JRR Tolkien, the distinguished Professor of Anglo-Saxon at Oxford and author of *The Lord of the Rings*, who sadly decided to remain at Oxford). New prefabricated huts began to spring up all over the grounds to house the sections created to

ENIGMA

The Enigma cipher machine was similar in appearance to a typewriter set in a metal or wooden box. The operator set his machine to an agreed setting and typed his message letter by letter on the machine's keys. This sent an electric impulse through a series of three rotating wheels to produce the enciphered letter, which lit up on a lampboard above the machine. After enciphering each letter, the first wheel rotated once, with the other wheels rotating after a varying number of letters to ensure that the enciphered version of each letter was constantly changing. The operator at the other end set his machine to the same original key settings and typed in the enciphered message. Each letter of the plain text then lit up on its lampboard.

RIGHT Wrens operating the Colossus, the first programmable electronic computer, used to break German enciphered teleprinter communications.

work on the various codes and ciphers. The paramount need for security, to protect the precious secret that the British were breaking the Enigma cipher, led the new sections to be known only by the name of the hut in which they were housed. German army and Luftwaffe Enigma ciphers were broken in Hut 6, while the German navy Enigma was broken in Hut 8.

Bletchley Park's first break into Enigma traffic occurred in December 1939, when Turing managed to crack five days of pre-war German navy Enigma, but it was not until 17 January 1940, during a visit by Turing to see the Poles, now evacuated to the French army codebreaking base near Paris, that the first wartime German army Enigma messages were deciphered. Bletchley broke the first message shortly after Turing's return, passing the results through to Hut 3, where deciphered German army and Luftwaffe messages were to be turned into MI6 "CX" reports which disguised them as intelligence collected by a mythical secret agent codenamed Boniface.

BELOW The Bombe was an electro-mechanical device designed by Alan Turing which tested possible solutions to Enigma messages to find the daily keys.

ALASTAIR DENNISTON

Alastair Denniston was in charge of the Admiralty's First World War codebreaking organization Room 40, named after the office in which it operated, and went on to take charge of the newly formed Government Code and Cipher School. His short stature and retiring nature led him to be described as "the little man" by subordinates who failed to recognize his great foresight. Denniston toured Britain's universities ahead of the Second World War "rounding up the dons" to work at Bletchley. He also pioneered the codebreaking alliance with the United States which remains critical to Britain's intelligence capabilities.

Referring to the recruitment of so many academics, particularly the mathematicians who led the way in breaking German ciphers, Josh Cooper, head of Bletchley Park's air section, said: "I have heard some cynics on the permanent staff scoffing at this. They did not realise that Denniston, for all his diminutive stature, was a bigger man than they."

Commander Travis.
Mr. ....
.... McVittie

SECRET.   CARELESS TALK.

66

24-8-40 1/3/2

From time to time, instances come to notice of careless talk on the part of members of the staff of this organisation.

Conversations about "Codes", "Cyphers" and "Machines" have been reported as taking place in restaurants and public houses.

A conversation, linking up Bletchley Park with the London address of H.Q. and another out-lying station, was overheard in an hotel. Enough was said to indicate clearly the close connection of the three establishments mentioned.

No conversation on service matters, however guarded, should ever take place in the hearing of persons not belonging to the organisation

It is impressed on all that irreparable damage may easily be caused by some trivial chance remark and the only safe rule is never to talk "shop" outside the office.

Heads of Sections are to read this notice to their Sections now and to each new member who may join their Section in the future.

D.C.S.S.
24th August, 1940.   A.G. Denniston

LEFT A memo from Alastair Denniston, the head of Bletchley Park, warning codebreakers that they should never talk about their work on German codes and ciphers.

MI5 AND THE SECOND WORLD WAR

MI5 grew out of the domestic section of the Secret Service Bureau set up in 1909 to deal with German spies coming into Britain.

ABOVE LEFT David Petrie, a former MI6 officer in the Middle East, who was MI5 director-general from April 1941 until the end of the war.

ABOVE RIGHT Guy Liddell, the Director of B Division, which hunted down German and Soviet spies during the war.

OPPOSITE Wormwood Scrubs prison was used by MI5 as its headquarters from August 1939 to May 1940. It then moved all its main departments to St James's St, London, and all others to Blenheim Palace in Oxfordshire.

It was run by Vernon Kell, an army officer with extensive service experience abroad, including a spell as war correspondent for *The Daily Telegraph* in China. MI5 was deemed as having had a good First World War, claiming in a shrewd piece of public relations to have rounded up all the German spies in Britain at the start of the war, although it subsequently transpired that some were not German spies at all, with one in fact being an agent working for the British Secret Intelligence Service (SIS).

Following the First World War, MI5 was initially restricted to maintaining security in the armed forces and, although during the 1930s it once again became responsible for domestic security operations against communist and fascist spies and saboteurs, it had just 36 officers on its books in July 1939. These included one spectacularly successful agent-runner, Maxwell Knight, who had previously worked for SIS and in the late 1930s successfully infiltrated the Communist Party of Great Britain for MI5, uncovering a Soviet spy ring at the Woolwich Arsenal, then Britain's explosives research centre.

By the start of the war, Kell was already 65 and soon demonstrated by his failure to prepare his service for the heavy workload that he was not the man for the job. Shortly before the outbreak of the Second World War, MI5 transferred its headquarters to Wormwood Scrubs prison in northwest London, but had far too few staff to cope with the joint threat from Nazi and Soviet spies and subversives.

There was one highlight in a successful operation by Maxwell Knight's section in infiltrating the far right; the uncovering of the leaking of secret communications between Winston Churchill, the British prime minister, and Franklin D Roosevelt, the American president, by Tyler Kent, a cipher clerk at the US embassy. These were being passed by a right-wing activist, Anna Wolkoff, a dressmaker for the Duchess of Windsor, to Berlin, via an Italian contact. The affair fuelled fears of attempts to replace King George VI with his elder brother the Duke of Windsor and install a government willing to make peace with Hitler.

Despite the success of the operation, new Prime Minister Winston Churchill was extremely concerned over the number of German, Austrian and Italian nationals living in the United Kingdom, many of whom were in fact refugees from their own countries and unlikely to be part of the "fifth column"

of fascist activists which he believed existed. Churchill was singularly unimpressed by Kell personally and more generally by MI5's failure to carry out the "very large round-up" of foreign nationals he believed was vital to safeguarding Britain's security. Churchill set up a Security Executive, chaired by Lord Swinton, a Conservative politician and former air minister, to ensure that MI5 was operating efficiently and to determine "whether there is a fifth column in this country and if there is eliminate it". The result was widespread internment, with around 26,000 Germans, Austrians and later Italians held in camps. There was a public outcry, not least because many of those who now found themselves interned had fled their own countries for the "freedom" of Britain. MI5 found itself blamed for the whole affair. Churchill, who had initially encouraged "a very large round-up", began to have serious doubts over the political wisdom of what he now described as "the witch-finding activities of MI5". The Home Office ruled that each and every internee should be investigated by MI5 with a view to releasing as many as possible.

By now MI5 had moved out of Wormwood Scrubs, with some departments moving to St James's Street and others less actively involved in the war itself based at Blenheim Palace in Oxfordshire. Impossibly overloaded by the increased workload caused by internment, the MI5 system broke down completely. Swinton blamed Kell and his palpable lack of preparation for war for the chaos that ensued. The hapless Kell was then summarily sacked on Churchill's orders. For six months MI5 was in disarray, with Jasper Harker, Kell's replacement, incapable of imposing his control or of fighting off attempts by Swinton to impose his own ideas of what the service should be.

The chaos within the first 18 months of the war had disastrous consequences, and not just for MI5 and those wrongly interned. MI5 completely failed to spot the Soviet infiltration by the Cambridge spy ring of British intelligence, with Guy Burgess and Kim Philby joining MI6 and John Cairncross working first at Bletchley Park and subsequently in MI6. Perhaps most embarrassingly of all, MI5 appointed Anthony Blunt to a senior post within its own organization. He lost no time in ensuring he had access to all the material collected by the MI5 Soviet counter-espionage section based at Blenheim Palace.

Concerned over the continuing chaos within MI5, Churchill asked Sir David Petrie, a retired Indian police officer who had been in charge of the intelligence in Delhi, to take over. Petrie was scathing of the effect of Swinton's interference and refused to take over as director-general unless he was allowed

MAXWELL KNIGHT (1900–1968)

Maxwell Knight joined the Royal Navy during the First World War, aged just 16. After the war he became Director of Intelligence of the British *Fascisti*, an ultra-right wing group, setting up his own agents within left-wing groups. He spent a brief period running these agents for MI6, which then had a role investigating "Bolshevism" in the UK, and subsequently for MI5. After the Second World War, Knight presented a BBC radio programme on nature for children as "Uncle Max", but his fame within the intelligence services was based on a willingness to wait years for the "sleeper" agents he placed inside the Communist Party to gain positions of influence. "The secret of his success was his uncanny ability at getting on with people," one former intelligence officer said. "He could persuade them to do things they didn't want to do, which is the secret of being a good agent-runner."

to be "master in his own house". Churchill agreed and Petrie took over in April 1941. A good man-manager, he set about rebuilding MI5.

Despite the multiple failures of the early years of the war, under Petrie's management MI5 went on to redeem itself; Maxwell Knight continued to enjoy success using Hunt's, an agency providing domestic staff to embassies in London, to infiltrate those of a number of countries, some of them British allies. Whenever Hunt's had a request for staff from one of the embassies where MI5 needed an agent, one run by Knight's M Section was placed in the post. The top target was the Spanish embassy because of its tacit support for Germany, but agents were even placed in the embassies of Britain's Belgian and Polish allies. MI5's greatest success, however, was its lead role in what is now widely recognized as one of the most brilliant espionage operations of all time, the Double Cross system.

ABOVE "Collar the Lot".
Under Churchill's orders,
thousands of Germans
and Austrians, many
of them Jews who had
fled Nazi Germany, were
incarcerated for the
duration of the war.

SIR VERNON KELL (1873–1942)

Vernon Kell was an officer in the South Staffordshire Regiment who had studied
Russian in Moscow and Chinese in Shanghai, where in 1900 he became caught up
in the Boxer uprising and reported as a war correspondent for *The Daily Telegraph*.
He was also an interpreter in French and German. In 1909,
amid major spy scares, Kell, now a captain, was made the
War Office representative on the Secret Service Bureau. He
headed the domestic security section of the bureau, while his
naval colleague Mansfield Cumming took charge of the foreign
intelligence section. The two sections soon split off, with Kell's
section becoming first MO5(g) and then, at the start of 1917,
acquiring the title MI5 by which it is now widely known. Kell ran
MI5 throughout the inter-war years, but prepared badly for the
Second World War and was sacked by Churchill in June 1940.

SPECIAL OPERATIONS EXECUTIVE (SOE)

The Special Operations Executive (SOE) grew out of a mix of the need to support resistance movements on the ground in countries occupied by Germany and Italy, and mistrust and suspicion within the military over the role played by Section D, the MI6 section set up shortly before the war to conduct sabotage operations behind enemy lines.

Despite the generals' opposition to a military force run by MI6 over which they had no control, relations were good between Section D, run by Major Lawrence Grand, and MIR (Military Intelligence Research), a small army staff team working on guerrilla warfare. This was in part because both Grand and Major JCF "Jo" Holland, who ran MIR, were Royal Engineer officers, and in part because their slightly different roles were compatible to the extent that, alongside his responsibilities as head of MIR, Holland was the military liaison with Section D.

In July 1940, within weeks of becoming Prime Minister, Winston Churchill ordered the creation of a single Special Operations Executive (SOE) which would provide resistance fighters with the training, assistance and leadership they needed to "set Europe ablaze".

The SOE absorbed Section D, MIR and Electra House (EH), a Foreign Office-controlled propaganda organization. The EH propaganda element became SO1, Section D became SO2 and MIR became the headquarters and planning organization SO3, which consisted of a number of "country sections" specializing in various areas. Stewart Menzies, the chief of MI6, believed that he would retain control of the SO2 element and was highly aggrieved to discover this was not the case. The three divisions disappeared in August 1941 when the propaganda arm SO1 was removed from SOE and renamed the Political Warfare Executive. SOE was deliberately placed under a separate ministry to both MI6 and the army, with Hugh Dalton, the minister of economic warfare, its main advocate, taking control of it. By placing it under Dalton's control, Churchill neatly ensured that it did not get smothered at birth by either Menzies or the generals. Dalton believed that the aim of SOE teams in the field should be "to co-ordinate, inspire, control and assist" any resistance group operating behind enemy lines, a concept embodied in SOE's official role "to co-ordinate all action, by way of subversion and sabotage, against the enemy overseas".

Operations were run from SOE headquarters, which was based in Michael House – the pre- and post-war headquarters of Marks and Spencer – at 64, Baker Street in London, its presence disguised by a plaque announcing that it was the home of the Inter-Services Research Bureau. It was led initially by Frank Nelson, a former Conservative MP, who before the war was British vice-consul (and MI6 representative) in Basle, and then from mid-1942 to September 1943 by the banker Charles Hambro. From late 1940 onwards, the most important figure

LEFT Former MI6 spy George Hill, who taught agents sabotage and became SOE representative in Moscow.

OPPOSITE Major-General Colin McVean Gubbins (centre), SOE chief of operations from November 1940 and head of SOE from September 1943, with Hugh Dalton, the minister for economic affairs, and Czech troops, Warwickshire, 1941.

within SOE was the director of operations and training, Major-General Colin Gubbins, an expert in irregular warfare who had practical experience in operations against the IRA in Ireland and the Bolsheviks in Russia. He was author of the army's manual on guerrilla warfare, and had spent the first year of the war working with the Czech and Polish forces who had men on the ground inside their own countries. Gubbins took over complete control from Hambro in September 1943.

Gubbins enjoyed a bitter rivalry with Menzies for much of the war. The relationship between the two – in part a result of Menzies' fury at the loss of control over Section D – reflected similar rivalries on the ground between MI6 officers, who naturally wanted the least possible attention directed towards their operations, and their SOE counterparts, whose raison d'être required that they created murder and mayhem, which inevitably attracted the attention of the German occupying forces. MI6 saw the SOE officers as upstarts who did not know what they were doing, while the SOE regarded many MI6 officers as incompetents more at home in the clubs of St James's than on the ground. Initially at least, both views had some justification. It is easy to exaggerate turf wars between secret organizations, but the rivalry between SOE and MI6 was at times so bitter as to be impossible to overstate. Nevertheless, there were a lot of good

SECTION D

MI6 carried out a number of special operations sabotage missions in Germany during the First World War and in Russia after the 1917 Bolshevik Revolution, so it was natural that Hugh Sinclair, the head of MI6, should establish a sabotage unit as part of his preparations for the Second World War. Set up on 1 April 1938, under Lieutenant-Colonel Lawrence Grand, it was officially designated Section IX but swiftly became known as Section D – the D standing quite literally for destruction. During the Munich crisis of September 1938, Section D set up a sabotage network in the Skoda armaments factories in Czechoslovakia, sent officers into the Balkans with the intention of sabotaging German access to oil and recruited an agent inside the Romanian oil industry. But the only significant sabotage carried out before the war was caused by army officers sent into Romania in civilian clothes, who disrupted rail supplies to Germany by putting sand in the axle boxes of trains.

"finishing school" was at Beaulieu House in Hampshire, where they were taught the tradecraft of the secret agent. SOE also had a number of "experimental establishments" working on developing a variety of secret equipment, ranging from exploding rats to sten guns concealed in pieces of wood and grenades hidden inside papier-mâché fruit.

The main SOE areas of operation were initially in East Africa, France, the Low Countries, Scandinavia, Poland, Czechoslovakia, the Balkans, North Africa and the Middle East, with limited operations in South America and West Africa. It expanded into the Far East after Japan's invasion of Malaya in December 1941. SOE also had a foothold in the United States where it was part of British Security Coordination, an organization headed by William Stephenson, the MI6 station chief, which also acted as liaison for both SOE and MI5 with their US counterparts. In the case of MI5, this was the FBI. In the case of SOE, it was the Office of Strategic Services, which combined both the SOE and the MI6 roles. SOE took some time to find its feet and the distrust of its operations was not confined to MI6. The organization's location led to SOE being nicknamed "the Baker Street Irregulars" after the gang of street urchins used by Sherlock Holmes for watching criminals. A naval intelligence history of the war described SOE as "a little blinded by the cloak and dazzled by the dagger", adding, "some time was to pass before the fierce young animal became house-trained".

officers in both organizations and in many cases the co-operation on the ground was, often out of pure necessity, much better than it was in London.

SOE had a number of training organizations, some of which were dedicated to training resistance fighters for specific countries, but potential SOE agents were taught guerrilla tactics at Arisaig in Inverness-shire – where they also learned "the art of silent killing" from former Shanghai policeman Major Bill Fairburn. Sabotage and the use of explosives was taught at Brickendonbury in Hertfordshire and agents learned how to drop by parachute behind enemy lines at RAF Ringway, near Manchester. The

COLIN MCVEAN GUBBINS   (1896–1976)

Colin Gubbins served in the Royal Field Artillery during the First World War and then as an intelligence officer during the Russian Intervention of 1919 and the Irish rebellion in the early 1920s. The last two tours led him to develop ideas for the use of special operations, which he expounded in a series of training manuals written shortly before the Second World War. From August 1939 until May 1940, Gubbins worked with the Czechs, the Poles and the Norwegians, preparing them for resistance. He then spent

several months creating the Auxiliary Units, which were to be the backbone of a British resistance if Germany invaded the United Kingdom. Gubbins then joined SOE, first as director of operations and later its head. He proved to be an inspirational and highly effective orchestrator of resistance in enemy-occupied territory. General Dwight D Eisenhower, Allied commander during the invasion of Europe, estimated that the contribution of the French Resistance alone had been worth six divisions.

ABOVE LEFT The SOE "finishing school" at Beaulieu known as "the House in the Woods" where the agents received their main training in how to operate behind enemy lines.

OPPOSITE SOE Mk III agent suitcase wireless set used by agents parachuted behind enemy lines in France and the Balkans.

NAVAL INTELLIGENCE

OPPOSITE The most important role of naval intelligence was tracking the U-boats to protect the Atlantic convoys.

The central focus of the Admiralty's Naval Intelligence Division (NID) during the Second World War was the Operational Intelligence Centre (OIC), which was based in the underground Citadel in Horse Guards Parade and tracked the passage of enemy ships and submarines.

Its sources were initially limited. Admiral John Godfrey, Director of Naval Intelligence for the first four years of the war, recalled that one officer sent to the Black Sea to observe Russian naval movements, "ended up in a Braila nightclub defying the Romanian Gestapo with a pistol in each hand. It was only by the personal intervention of the British minister that he was smuggled out". At one point, the NID even devised a scheme to predict what Hitler might do next by having astrological charts drawn up for him, since "it had been known for some time that Hitler attached importance to astrological advice".

But by mid-1941, the breaking by Bletchley Park of the Enigma ciphers of the Kriegsmarine (German navy), supplemented by human intelligence from MI6 agents and coastal watchers in Scandinavia and France, was enabling the OIC to track the bulk of German warships and re-route the allied convoys bringing vital supplies across the Atlantic to avoid German submarines, or U-boats. Although there was a damaging 10-month blackout in Bletchley's coverage of the U-boat ciphers from March 1942 owing to the introduction by the Kriegsmarine of a new four-rotor Enigma machine, codenamed Shark, thereafter the NID knew where every U-boat was on a daily basis.

Godfrey's personal staff officer and link-man with MI6, Bletchley Park and SOE was Ian Fleming, who drew on his experience during the war in his creation of James Bond, not least in making Bond a commander in the Royal Naval Volunteer Reserve like himself, although Fleming's personal designation NI17f does not have quite the ring of 007. Fleming proved to be a staunch defender of MI6 during the early years of the war when Godfrey was co-ordinating criticism of its intelligence reporting on behalf not just of the NID, but also the military intelligence and air intelligence departments. When a March 1940 report by the former cabinet secretary Lord Hankey largely exonerated MI6 of any significant failings, Godfrey pushed for the navy to create its own secret service. but Fleming advised against it, warning that if MI6 were sidelined there would be "a grave danger of letting the baby out with the bath water". He recommended instead that Godfrey "infiltrate" his own men into MI6. "I think that the infusion of new blood into the existing organisation would be better than chopping off hoary but experienced heads," Fleming said. He even went so far as to suggest that "C", the head of MI6, Stewart Menzies, should have "a young staff officer" to advise him in the same way that he himself advised Godfrey. Fleming's recommendation was taken up by Godfrey and the three service intelligence chiefs were subsequently allowed to appoint their own personal representatives to be part of the MI6 management, while a Foreign Office representative was appointed as C's personal adviser.

As a result of his position both as Godfrey's staff officer and his liaison with MI6, SOE and Bletchley, Fleming was at the heart of much of what naval intelligence did during the war. As might be expected of the creator of James Bond, he was an inveterate inventor of imaginative secret missions and during the so-called "Shark Blackout" in 1942, he devised a plan codenamed Operation Ruthless to try to snatch one

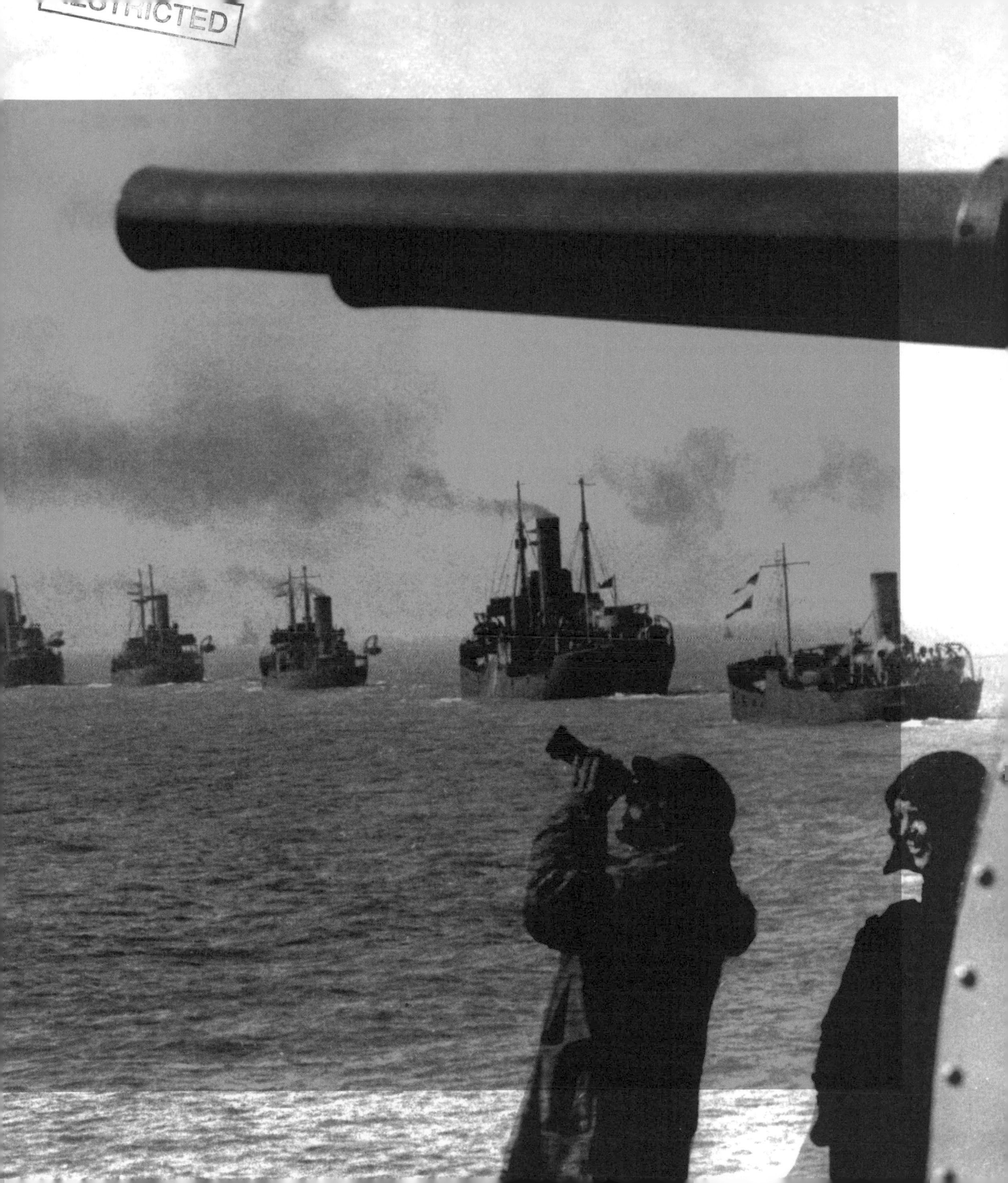
ESTRICTED

of the new Enigma machines in use by the U-Boats. He also created a unit of Royal Marines, 30 Assault Unit, to launch raids on enemy positions to collect intelligence and material such as codebooks and cipher keys that would help the Bletchley codebreakers.

Another of Fleming's schemes was codenamed Operation Goldeneye, subsequently the title of one of the Bond films. It was originally a set of plans to carry out operations in Spain should the Germans invade, but swiftly focused on the protection of Gibraltar, which was central to British ability to control entry to the Mediterranean. Naval intelligence took the lead on secret service operations in Spain, with Captain Alan Hillgarth, the naval attaché in the British Embassy in Madrid, representing the interests not just of naval intelligence but also MI6 and SOE.

Gibraltar was the key to the Mediterranean and a major part of Operation Goldeneye involved a stay-behind team to be based in tunnels dug out of the rock. The tunnels were hewn out of the rock with ventilation shafts, a 38,000-litre (10,000-gallon) water-tank installed, and a clandestine wireless station set up so that the stay-behind team could report on German naval movements. Fleming drew up a survival manual including details of weapons should the team need to defend their lair as well as the best types of food and medical supplies, even setting down which types of clothes to wear and the need for a large number of books to read. Plan Tracer, as the Gibraltar stay-behind team was known, never came to fruition. Nor did defence chiefs accept Fleming's suggestion that the SOE should be sent into Spain to destroy the German infra-red detection system set up at Algeciras to detect Royal Navy ships going in and out of the Mediterranean.

Kim Philby, then in charge of MI6 counter-espionage operations covering Spain, later recalled he also considered the use of SOE, adding in an apparent dig at Fleming that "I doubted that anyone on our side would really welcome a James-Bond-like free-for-all in Spain". Instead, the British ambassador to Spain, Sir Samuel Hoare, protested to the Spanish government at the breach of its neutrality in allowing the Abwehr (German military intelligence) to place infra-red devices on Spanish territory and Berlin was forced to remove them. Goldeneye was subsequently the title of the seventeenth James Bond film, but it was never used by Fleming for any of the Bond stories or books. Nevertheless, he clearly had an affection for it, using it as the name for his post-war home in Jamaica.

LEFT Frank Birch, the actor and stage director who was head of the Bletchley Park naval section.

OPPOSITE Fleming devised a plan to place an observation team in tunnels dug into the rock of Gibraltar to spy on the Germans if they ever managed to capture it.

A number of other elements of Fleming's wartime intelligence work did in fact make it into the Bond books. During a trip to Washington with Godfrey, they stopped off in Lisbon, where Fleming heard that the local Abwehr chief was fond of using the casino at Estoril. Fleming went there hoping to beat the German spymaster at his favourite card game Chemin de Fer. Sadly, Fleming was not as successful as Bond was to be in the 1953 novel *Casino Royale* when he bankrupts the villain le Chiffre. He lost far more than the £50 in expenses he had on him and had to be bailed out by Godfrey.

ALAN HILLGARTH (1899–1978)

Hillgarth was the eighth generation of his family to join the Royal Navy. In 1911, at the age of 12, he entered the Royal Naval College, Osborne, where one of his tutors was Alastair Denniston, later head of Bletchley Park. He retired from the navy in 1927 to write highly successful adventure novels and was appointed British vice-consul in Majorca, subsequently becoming consul. When the Second World War broke out, Admiral John Godfrey, Director of Naval Intelligence, had Hillgarth appointed naval attaché to co-ordinate intelligence operations in Spain. Hillgarth's contacts with Juan March, one of the wealthiest men in Spain and an influential voice in the Fascist camp, allowed him to pay a large number of bribes to Franco and his generals to limit Spain's support for Germany and the facilities provided to it in terms of use of ports and intelligence facilities.

ROL OF NAVAL SEC

lligence may be

es (agents).

tion.

g.

naissance.

H.M. Ships, and

es, Reporting Of
above ground" or

requirement of N

th accurate and

ents of the Germ

rtant requiremen

building program
d submarines.

l technical deve

f German shippin
coasts and in an

Great War the N
was then the Coa
al reconnaissanc
the war and alth
rate head, in ef
ary funds and o

s of economy I b
stguards, was ha
erial reconna
war and was clo
onsibility of th

ADMIRAL JOHN GODFREY

(1888–1971)

John Godfrey joined the Royal Navy in 1903 and served through the First World War and inter-war years, mainly at sea, before being appointed Director of Naval Intelligence in February 1939. He worked tirelessly preparing for the war, encouraging attempts to improve the intelligence provide by MI6 and setting up the Operational Intelligence Centre (OIC) which tracked the movement of enemy warships and submarines, primarily to protect the Atlantic convoys bringing supplies to the United Kingdom. He set up the Inter-Service Topographical Department (ISTD) based at Oxford, which collected photographs of coastlines worldwide, including holiday photographs, to assist in the preparation of landings by spies, saboteurs or larger military forces. Godfrey also played a key role in the development of the Joint Intelligence Committee, which still assesses and reports on the intelligence produced by all the secret agencies today.

**THESE PAGES AND
FOLLOWING PAGES**

A November 1939 report
from John Godfrey, Director
of Naval Intelligence, criticizing
MI6 for the lack of intelligence
it is producing.

<u>D.C.N.S.</u>

<u>CONTROL OF NAVAL SECRET SERVICE.</u>

Naval intelligence may be **derived** from -

(a) Secret sources (agents).

(b) Cryptography.

(c) D/F interception.

(d) Coastwatching.

(e) Aerial reconnaissance.

(f) Reports from H.M. Ships, and merchant ships.

(g) Naval Attaches, Reporting Officers, S.O's(I),
     and other "above ground" organisations.

2.   The <u>chief</u> requirement of Naval Intelligence is to
provide the C.N.S. with accurate and up to date news of the
whereabouts and movements of the German Navy.

3.   Other important requirements are -

(a) German shipbuilding programme, especially
     BISMARCK and submarines.

(b) German Naval technical developments, mines etc.

(c) Movements of German shipping, especially on
     Norwegian coasts and in and out of the Belts
     and Sound.

4.   Before the Great War the Navy controlled its coast
watching service; it was then the Coastguards. The Secret Service,
Cryptography and aerial reconnaissance were non-existent. These
were built up during the war and although the Secret Service was
normally under a separate head, in effect Admiral Hall had the
disposal of the necessary funds and controlled his own system of
agents abroad.

5.   For reasons of economy I believe the coast watching
service, then the Coastguards, was handed over to the Board of
Trade before the war. Aerial reconnaissance was handed over to
the R.A.F. after the war and was closely followed by cryptography,
which became the responsibility of the Foreign Office. The

Secret /

Secret Service was allowed to die and was later resuscitated
mildly as an organisation controlled by the Foreign Office.
Thus the extraordinary paradox, without example in any other
Navy, that none of our important sources of intelligence,
except D/F interception, reports from H.M. Ships and the above
ground Attache, S.O.(I) organisation, are under the control of
the C.N.S.   The important ones, the Secret Service, Cryptography,
aerial reconnaissance and coast watching have been deliberately
handed over to other Government Departments.   We thus find
ourselves in the position of being unable to do anything much to
improve these services although they contribute vitally towards
the success of Naval operations.   We can ask them for
information, we can criticise them and encourage them, but only
by very indirect means and with the exercise of great tact can we
arrive at any conclusion regarding their efficiency.

6.   In the past the policy has been to make the best of
a bad job and I have hesitated to draw attention to the
shortcomings of the Secret Service until war experience gave us
some lead .   After three months of war I can confidently
say that we are not getting the information we need, and as far
as I can see under the present organisation there is little
likelihood that we shall.

7.   I find myself with deep regret unable to tell the
Board anything of value about the German shipbuilding programme,
or about the development of German weapons - the magnetic mine
is a case in point.   Although the problem is a simple one and
was solved during the Great War, we have little information from
the Secret Service regarding German movements in and out of the
Baltic. Such as we have is derived from the French service
through the British Naval Attache, Copenhagen.

A /

A simultaneous picture of the ships present in German harbours is rarely obtainable, and it is literally impossible to co-ordinate things so that we can achieve a simultaneous aerial reconnaissance and "account" by agents. Our lack of information about movements on the Norwegian coasts has frequently called for comment and criticism and rightly so. The pooling of Secret Service activities under one head in each country has inevitably led to political news being given priority and the Naval service has become a Cinderella. The arrest of Mr. Stevens and Mr. Best on the Dutch frontier has completely disrupted all political, Military and Naval intelligence through Holland and has brought our modest Naval organisation to an abrupt end - it is unlikely to revive. Such information as we glean in future will be through the French.

8.   My trip to the Baltic immediately before the war in which I came into personal contact with all the head agents convinced me that although they were very worthy and keen, they had no knowledge of Naval or maritime needs, with the exception of the representative at Stockholm who happened to be a Naval Officer. All the others were soldiers or civilians and chiefly occupied on political work.

The headquarters office in England contains a number of Naval Officers but the majority have been retired for many years and have lost touch with Naval realities. The "control" is mainly in the hands of ex-soldiers.

9.   Our relations with this organisation are excellent and I have never received anything but the greatest kindness and consideration from them all. Admiral Sinclair particularly always went out of his way to help me, but lately he inevitably became absorbed in political work and our Naval needs could only receive cursory attention.

In /

10.   In a paper submitted the other day I proposed certain palliatives (see attached Memorandum), but on further consideration I feel that these are only half measures and that the organisation is unlikely in its present form to give us the sort of intelligence we need.   Neither am I particularly sanguine that in Germany it will be able to secure the necessary penetration unless it has been established firmly in peace time.   This does not apply in other countries where new lines can be developed and may subsequently lead to intelligence encirclement of Germany being more complete.   In such countries as Spain, Mexico and South America much can be done if money is available.

11.   Admiral Hall, who knows more than any living man about Naval intelligence, is deeply concerned at the situation that has arisen.   He can explain the difficulties and possibilities far better than I and feels that the First Lord and C.N.S. will not receive the information they need unless and until they assume control of the organisation which produces it.   By doing this they will reproduce the situation which in effect existed during most of the Great War, although it was never officially recognised.   Might I suggest that Admiral Hall be asked his opinion on this vitally important matter before any decision regarding the future of the Secret Service is made?

D.   N.   I.
30/11/39

THESE PAGES A draft memo from John Godfrey, Director of Naval Intelligence, to Stewart Menzies, the "chief" of MI6, outlining his complaints. It is drafted by Ian Fleming, the creator of James Bond, and signed by him as "F".

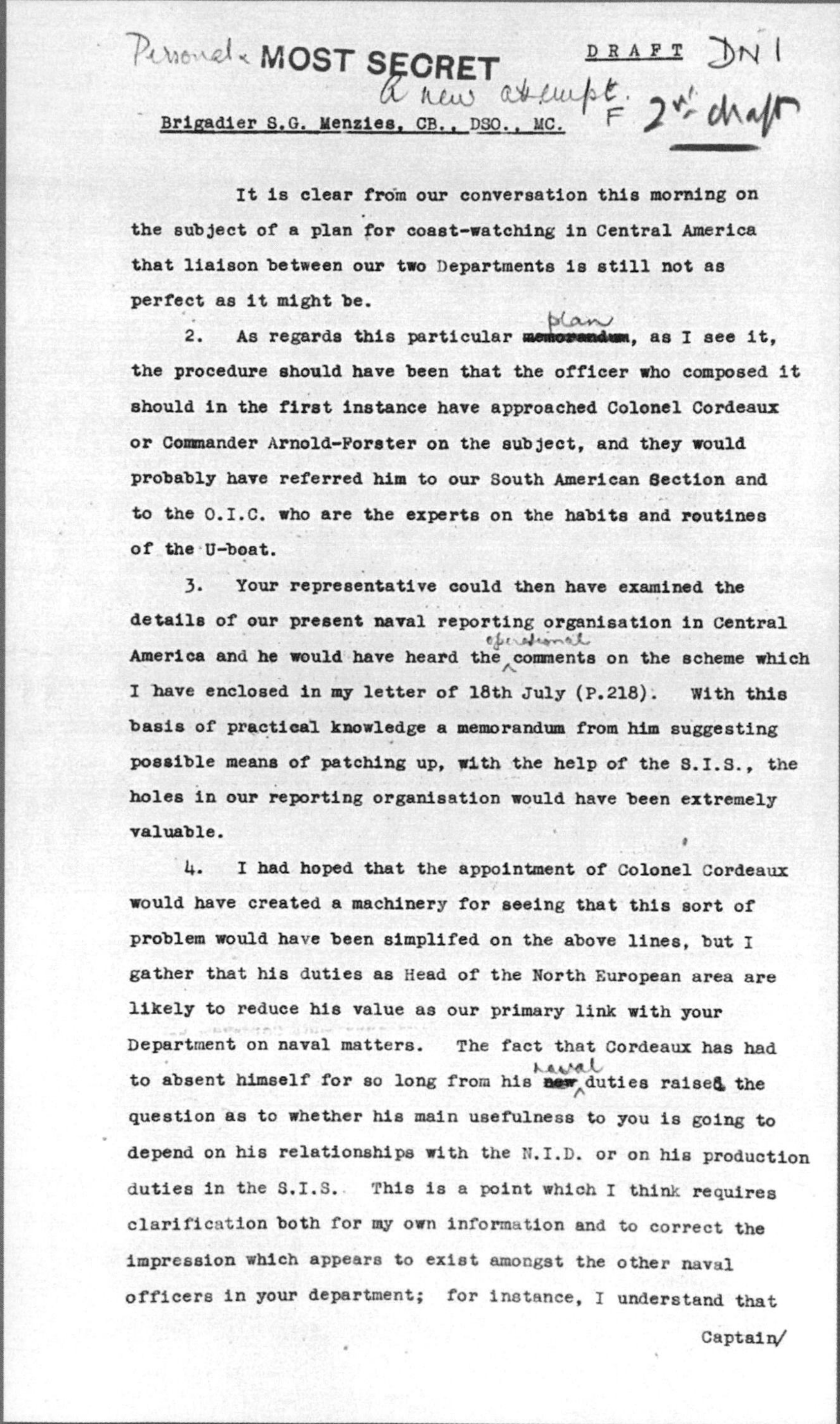

Personal – **MOST SECRET** DRAFT DNI

A new attempt. F 2nd draft

Brigadier S.G. Menzies, CB., DSO., MC.

It is clear from our conversation this morning on the subject of a plan for coast-watching in Central America that liaison between our two Departments is still not as perfect as it might be.

2. As regards this particular ~~memorandum~~ plan, as I see it, the procedure should have been that the officer who composed it should in the first instance have approached Colonel Cordeaux or Commander Arnold-Forster on the subject, and they would probably have referred him to our South American Section and to the O.I.C. who are the experts on the habits and routines of the U-boat.

3. Your representative could then have examined the details of our present naval reporting organisation in Central America and he would have heard the operational comments on the scheme which I have enclosed in my letter of 18th July (P.218). With this basis of practical knowledge a memorandum from him suggesting possible means of patching up, with the help of the S.I.S., the holes in our reporting organisation would have been extremely valuable.

4. I had hoped that the appointment of Colonel Cordeaux would have created a machinery for seeing that this sort of problem would have been simplifed on the above lines, but I gather that his duties as Head of the North European area are likely to reduce his value as our primary link with your Department on naval matters. The fact that Cordeaux has had to absent himself for so long from his ~~new~~ naval duties raised the question as to whether his main usefulness to you is going to depend on his relationships with the N.I.D. or on his production duties in the S.I.S. This is a point which I think requires clarification both for my own information and to correct the impression which appears to exist amongst the other naval officers in your department; for instance, I understand that

Captain/

- 2 -

Captain Russell is to deputise for Colonel Cordeaux in his absence but is at the same time extremely chary of making decisions when he is away, and the fact that Colonel Cordeaux has arranged for all naval matters to be canalised through him or his deputy has tended to put a curb on the initiative of other members of the Naval Section.

5.   Curiously enough, Cordeaux's appointment has thus in some respects lessened the direct liaison between our Departments on a lower level.   This tendency has not been so apparent during his absence in Stockholm and things are now working fairly normally again, i.e. Arnold-Forster is in direct touch with D.D.N.I., Fleming, and Heads of Sections, and Commander   is always available.   Captain Russell maintains his daily visits as previously.

6.   I should greatly deplore any weakening of the liaison on this level.   The fact that these channels were not used by Commander ~~Cowan~~ Cohen in forwarding his memorandum have been largely responsible for the confusion which subsequently resulted.

7.   I would be very grateful if you could think over the points I have raised and let me have your views.   The issue in a nutshell is whether Colonel Cordeaux ~~should~~ can combine his production duties for a certain part of Europe with ~~our~~ day-to-day requirements ~~affecting naval relationships with~~ your organisation throughout the world.

F

21.7.42.

ABOVE Ian Fleming, the creator of James Bond, was Godfrey's assistant, playing a vital role in liaising between naval intelligence and both MI6 and Bletchley Park.

MILITARY INTELLIGENCE

The Directorate of Military Intelligence expanded radically at the start of the war and a number of new sections were created in a reorganization in 1940.

ABOVE Captain Thomas Kendrick, pre-war MI6 head of station in Vienna, who worked for MI19 interrogating high-grade German prisoners of war.

OPPOSITE The journalist and broadcaster Malcolm Muggeridge was recruited into the Intelligence Corps, later working for MI6 in Mozambique.

The most important of these were MI8, which controlled military participation in signals intelligence, both in the interception of enemy wireless messages and the analysis and reporting of intelligence from communications intercepted by mobile stations during military operations; MI9, which gathered intelligence from prisoners of war; and MI14, a special section concentrating on building up a complete picture of German military formations from all available sources. MI5 remained the section liaising with the Security Service, while for the first time MI6 was used for liaison with the Secret Intelligence Service, giving SIS the title by which it would become much better known.

The start of the war also saw the formal creation of the army's Intelligence Corps, which had existed during the First World War, but only as a loose collection of officers and soldiers who remained members of their original corps and regiments. Under persistent lobbying from Major WF Jeffries, the officer responsible for military intelligence personnel, the War Office finally agreed to the creation of an independent Intelligence Corps, approved by King George VI in July 1940. Jeffries was appointed as its first commandant.

"Intelligence, with all its ramifications and duties, became so vast and grew up so rapidly that I felt it was impossible to control properly or obtain that esprit de corps which was essential," he said. "I had numerous talks with the late Brigadier Martin (the Deputy Director of Military Intelligence) and with General Frederick Beaumont-Nesbitt (the Direction of Military Intelligence) pleading for a corps. Both agreed on the necessity, but masses of difficulties arose, chiefly as to where a proper and large enough building and training ground could be obtained. I asked for Holloway College, Virginia Water, which would have been ideal, but was told that the education of women could not be interfered with!" Nevertheless, using private connections, Jeffries succeeded in acquiring two Oxford colleges, Oriel and Pembroke, as a corps headquarters and officer training centre, while other ranks were trained at King Alfred's College, Winchester.

The journalist and broadcaster Malcolm Muggeridge, one of those who joined the new corps, recalled the "ill-concealed distaste and disdain" with which he and his colleagues, "mostly schoolmasters, journalists, encyclopaedia salesmen, unfrocked clergymen and other displaced *New Statesman* readers" were regarded. Members of the new corps were recruited by more subtle means than some of their fellow soldiers, recalled David Engleheart, who joined up in 1940, shortly after the corps was formed. "Having been brought up on Buchan's Richard Hannay novels, there was a certain romance in answering an advertisement in the personal column of *The Daily Telegraph* in 1940 inviting one to apply to a box number if one spoke foreign languages and wished to serve one's country," Engleheart recalled. "Spice was added on discovering that the address for the subsequent assignation was the legendary shop at the Trafalgar Square end of Northumberland Avenue. Upstairs to a door opened by a bespectacled corporal and into an untidy room presided over by an unmistakably schoolmasterly captain, who, without ceremony, proceeded to give a few chaps and me a French *dictée* which was taken away to be corrected by the corporal. He then told us to confess to any pink, red or other political rashes into which we might have broken out during adolescence ('We will find out anyway'), said that we had volunteered for the Intelligence Corps and would be inducted at an undisclosed date." When he was finally called up, he discovered that his new colleagues were "a sophisticated mixture of intellectuals, world travellers, artists, journalists, film directors, jockeys, MPs – you name it they were there".

The main roles of the new Intelligence Corps were the collection of strategic intelligence from assessment of aerial photography and signals intelligence; the assimilation of tactical intelligence from a variety of sources – including both of the above plus forward reconnaissance, captured documents and the interrogation or debriefing of prisoners of war, agents and refugees – and counter-intelligence and security, of everything from documents to military bases, airfields, ports and even brothels. Debriefing one soldier who had reported information being freely circulated in a Middle East "knocking shop", Maurice Oldfield, then just an Intelligence Corps lieutenant, but later to become the chief of MI6, asked: "Couldn't you have stayed with the girl just a bit longer, until breakfast time, say? I'm sure she could have told you a lot more."

Interrogation of enemy prisoners was controlled by Lieutenant-Colonel Norman Crockatt. Initially Crockatt was head of MI9, an overarching prisoner-of-war (PoW) intelligence organization which also assisted British servicemen captured by the enemy to escape, debriefing them once they got out, and encouraged those still in PoW camps to provide intelligence via coded letters.

In 1942, in a further reorganization of military intelligence, MI9's operations were split into two separate organizations, with intelligence from British PoWs remaining as MI9 and interrogation of enemy PoWs becoming MI19. Interrogations took place at Combined Services Detailed Interrogation Centres (CSDIC) in the UK, in Cairo and in Delhi. The headquarters and main interrogation centre for enemy prisoners in Britain, known as "the London Cage", was based initially at Cockfosters Barracks, Trent Park, northeast London, before moving to new purpose-built centres at Latimer and Wilton Park, Beaconsfield, in Buckinghamshire. A number of German prisoners co-operated with their British captors. Others were infiltrated by "stool pigeons" or bugged in "Source X" operations. There were 30 purpose-built bugged rooms in each of the two camps, where prisoners expected to produce valuable intelligence were held in pairs with nothing to do apart from sleep or talk to each other while German-speaking operators listened in, working in shifts of six per room to ensure nothing was missed. The most famous German prisoner of war held by the British was Rudolf Hess, who flew to Britain in May 1941 in a misguided attempt to seek a peace between Britain and Nazi Germany.

ABOVE MI9 moved the Combined Services Detailed Interrogation Centre to Latimer and Wilton Park in Beaconsfield in 1943.

RIGHT Trent Park in Enfield, north London, the original site of MI19's main interrogation centre, known as "the London Cage".

AIR INTELLIGENCE

During the 1930s, the intelligence department of the Air Ministry was a relatively small one led by a retired army major, Archie Boyle, who had been in the department since the First World War.

A ir intelligence was poorly funded and suffered from a lack of support from senior air officers, with the result that on the outbreak of war there were far too few officers to provide the intelligence that was needed. Boyle was commissioned into the RAF at the start of the war and given the rank of air commodore. He was also put forward by the RAF as its candidate to head MI6 when Hugh Sinclair died, but pre-war failings of air intelligence led to his being dismissed as a sensible candidate for the post. Boyle was replaced in 1941 by Air Commodore Charles Medhurst, who was himself soon succeeded by Air Commodore Frank Inglis, who then remained Director of Air Intelligence for the rest of the war.

Prior to the war, air intelligence had persistently underestimated the strength of the Luftwaffe, disbelieving MI6 reports that contradicted the RAF's own estimates. One of the agents, run by Frank Foley, the MI6 station chief in Berlin, was a Luftwaffe colonel working in the German Air Ministry who volunteered his services in return for large amounts of cash. Given his access to high-grade intelligence from the office of Goering, the head of the Luftwaffe, and the panic in London over a claim by Hitler that the Luftwaffe had reached parity with the RAF, SIS agreed to pay him. His information was not regarded as credible in London, largely because it contradicted the more conservative estimates of the RAF. The Air Ministry simply dismissed it – a typical example of the difficulties MI6

INTELLIGENCE IN THE BATTLE OF BRITAIN

During the second half of 1940, the codebreakers at Bletchley Park began picking up ominous indications in Luftwaffe messages that a major German operation, codenamed Sea Lion, was being planned, and it soon became clear that this referred to the invasion of Britain. The Germans knew their troops would never get across the Channel unless they had complete air superiority, and so on 10 July 1940 the Luftwaffe launched the first of a series of sustained attacks on the United Kingdom. The resultant clash between their fighter escorts and the RAF's fighters in the skies over southern England became known as the Battle of Britain. Vital tactical intelligence on the planned raids came from the interception of Luftwaffe low-level communications by Cheadle and a network of small RAF radio-monitoring "Y" units co-ordinated from West Kingsdown in Kent. Bletchley gave advance notice of the planned times of raids, the intended targets and the numbers of aircraft involved, but these were often subject to unannounced changes. Its most important contribution was in providing accurate detail of the large German losses and in September the news that, as a result of these losses, Operation Sea Lion had effectively been abandoned.

faced in putting across information where the source could not be disclosed. The Air Ministry was wrong.

Over the next three years, Foley met the Luftwaffe officer every two weeks, regularly receiving photocopies of top-secret documents with details of both the structure of the rapidly expanding Luftwaffe and its strategy. But when Nevile Henderson, the British ambassador in Berlin, discovered where the information was coming from, Foley was ordered to drop his agent lest the Germans found out, another classic example of the problems MI6 faced with British ambassadors abroad.

One branch of air intelligence that was prepared for war was AI1c, the air intelligence section of MI6, led by Frederick Winterbotham. Given the lack of enthusiasm from senior RAF officers for intelligence, it took the initiative in what would become the RAF's main source of intelligence outside of the Bletchley Park material.

Winterbotham persuaded Sinclair to set up an air reconnaissance section in tandem with the French Deuxième Bureau. He recruited Sidney Cotton, an Australian pilot, who carried out a number of missions, some in co-operation with the French, to photograph border areas of Germany and Italian-occupied territory in the Mediterranean and East Africa. The first flight over Germany came in March 1939, when Cotton used a Leica camera to photograph Mannheim. During July and August, he flew his Lockheed 12A deep into German territory, under cover of a front company called the Aeronautical Research and Sales Corporation, and photographed a number of locations of interest to British intelligence, including Berlin and the German naval base at Wilhelmshafen. John Weaver, a member of Cotton's unit, described how, shortly before the

SCIENTIFIC INTELLIGENCE

A claim by Hitler in September 1939 that he had "a secret weapon" led air intelligence to attach a scientist to AI1c, the air section of MI6 led by Squadron-Leader Frederick Winterbotham. Professor R V Jones (below) analyzed the Oslo Report. This list of German technological developments was sent to the British embassy in Oslo by a German scientist grateful for the assistance of Frank Foley, the pre-war MI6 head of station in Berlin, in getting a young Jewish girl he knew out of Germany. It included details of two kinds of radar, one of which was already in use, a sample of a new electronic proximity fuse, and information on the development of the V1 and V2 rockets. Jones also worked out how to counter the German *Knickebein* bombing system which used two radio beams to direct the Luftwaffe bombers on to their target. The RAF used jammers to bend the beams and divert the bombers away from their targets. The German invention of new systems

and the subsequent British invention of new counter-measures became known as "the Battle of the Beams". Later in the war, Jones devised a scheme to divert the German V2 rockets away from their targets.

outbreak of war, Cotton flew to Berlin's Tempelhof airport: "Goering and his lieutenants were there. Seeing the aircraft, they made enquiries as to whom it belonged. On finding out, they approached Cotton for a flight and asked where he would take them. Cotton said: 'I have a dear old aunt who lives in such and such an area and if you have no objections we could fly over there.' It was agreed and off they set. But what they did not know was that dear old Sydney was pressing the tit the whole time, taking photographs."

Cotton offered his services to the RAF in August 1939, but was turned down, the RAF being "unsympathetic to irregular operations in general, and Cotton in particular". But within weeks the RAF had realized that Cotton was providing MI6 with valuable intelligence and insisted on taking over his operation. Cotton was commissioned as a wing commander in charge of the Photographic Development Unit at Heston, just west of London. Initially, the RAF tried to use Blenheim and Lysander aircraft, but they could not fly high or fast enough to evade the German fighters and eventually "Cottonized" Spitfires were used. Cotton himself continued to rub the RAF top brass up the wrong way. "He obtained what he wanted where he could get it; he was impatient of 'the usual channels'; he applied business methods to government officials and, instead of filling in forms, put them in the waste-paper basket," one officer said. "Nor did he hesitate to tell senior air officers who obstructed him precisely what he thought of them. The air

staff loathed him. Their opinion was that he was 'a line-shooter, racketeer and salesman who does not deliver the goods'." But the RAF needed the intelligence Cotton produced, which not only provided them with the locations of key targets, but could also be used after bombing raids to assess the results and indicate which targets needed to be revisited.

By mid-1940, demand for aerial photography had grown to such an extent that the services of "Cotton's Crooks" were no longer sufficient. The RAF gratefully used this as an excuse to dispense with him. The unit was re-christened 1 Photographic Reconnaissance Unit, and a separate Photographic Interpretation Unit was set up in the north-London suburb of Wembley. Within a year, the success of aerial reconnaissance led all three services to clamour for more, and the number of photo-reconnaissance aircraft was more than doubled, from 33 to 78. The introduction of Mosquitoes at the end of 1941 allowed vast areas of eastern Germany and the Baltic ports to be photographed and the development of more powerful cameras led to details of U-boat construction being studied for the first time. The Wembley interpretation unit moved to Danesfield House on the banks of the Thames at Medmenham in Buckinghamshire, where it became the Central Interpretation Unit. By 1944, no enemy-controlled area in Europe was beyond the RAF's range, making photographic intelligence one of the most widely used and important sources of intelligence.

The other main source of intelligence obtained by the RAF was signals intelligence. The RAF made much more extensive use of material from Bletchley Park than is widely recognized and had a large air section there, AI1f, run by the eccentric Josh Cooper; this was usually able to predict from the weather information sent on Luftwaffe radio nets which cities German bombers were aiming to attack, thereby ensuring sufficient fighters were in the air. The RAF also set up a scientific intelligence section run by Professor R V Jones, which found ways of jamming the radio beams the Luftwaffe used to guide its aircraft on to their targets.

THE EXILES, MI6'S INTELLIGENCE ALLIES

MI6 had a bad start to the war, as the German advances across Europe robbed it of many of its most important stations and agent networks.

LEFT Paul Thümmel, agent A54, a Gestapo officer run by Czechoslovak intelligence who provided vital information in the early part of the war.

OPPOSITE General František Moravec (left) the Czechoslovak intelligence chief who helped MI6, seen here with the wartime Czechoslovak leaders-in-exile.

The service was saved largely by a number of good liaison relationships with the intelligence organizations of the Polish, Czech, Norwegian and French governments-in-exile, and also with the Vichy French Deuxième Bureau, some of whose members were prepared to work with the British. By the end of 1941, this co-operation had extended the reach of MI6 considerably. One of the closest and most successful relationships, although at times it was also one of the most tense, was with the Poles, whose early work on the Enigma machine cipher had done so much to assist the Bletchley Park codebreakers.

The close links with Czech intelligence were formed before the war by the MI6 bureau chief in Prague, Harold "Gibby" Gibson, who smuggled the head of Czech intelligence, General František Moravec, out of the country before the March 1939 German invasion. The Czechs had a number of agents inside Germany, including the particularly valuable Paul Thümmel, a senior Abwehr officer. Known to the British as agent A54, Thümmel provided comprehensive detail of German forces and intentions, including plans for the invasions of Poland, France, Britain and the USSR, before being detected by the Gestapo in October 1941.

There were also strong links with the Norwegian government-in-exile's intelligence department, FOII. Prior to the German invasion of Norway in April 1940, MI6 officers in Oslo led by Frank Foley, now better known for his role saving tens of thousands of Jews from Nazi Germany, had recruited a number of agents and set up coast-watching networks to report on the movement of German warships. After the invasion, MI6 made use of Norwegian fishing boats to ferry agents between Norway and the Shetland Islands in an operation run by Leslie Mitchell, Foley's former deputy in Berlin and Oslo, which became known as "the Shetland Bus" (see page 50). One Norwegian agent run by MI6 had such good contacts in Germany that he was given the run of German military facilities. The intelligence he supplied included the crucial report in May 1941 that allowed the Royal Navy to sink the latest German battleship, the *Bismarck*.

Relations between MI6 and the various French intelligence services were complicated by political rivalries. The Gaullist Bureau Central de Renseignements et d'Action set up a coast-watching operation in the French Atlantic ports and the *Confrérie de Notre Dame* agent network, which began in northwest France but expanded to cover much of the country. It was run by Gilbert Renault and until mid-1943, when it was rolled up by the Germans, provided useful intelligence including that which led to the British raid on the German radar station at Saint-Bruneval, north of Le Havre, and the capture of key components for scientific analysis. Thereafter, the Davis network, based around the Mediterranean port of Nice, was the most productive of any MI6 network in the six-month period

leading up to March 1944. The jewel in the crown was the Alliance network run from May 1941 by the beautiful Marie-Madeleine Fourcade. Her network was known to the Abwehr as Noah's Ark because it named its agents after animals. Fourcade was codenamed Hedgehog and she was particularly prickly for the Germans. Arrested in November 1942, she managed to escape to London and continued to run the network from a house in Chelsea.

Paradoxically, there was also a highly productive relationship with the Deuxième Bureau, which had worked closely with MI6 before the war, supplying the vital link to the Polish codebreakers, but which remained under the Vichy government. This was turned to an advantage when the bureau provided advanced warning of German round-ups of British agents and information on German and Italian troop movements from French ports to North Africa. During 1942, it was also able to obtain highly valuable intelligence on German operations in the Balkans and on the Eastern Front from Source K, Robert Keller, a French post-office engineer who tapped the German landline communications between Paris and Hitler's headquarters, the so-called "Wolf's Lair" just outside the East Prussian town of Rastenburg, now Kętrzyn in Poland.

But the best and most productive of the relationships with the European allies was with the Poles. While the most important aspect of this lay in the work of the young codebreakers who cracked the Enigma cipher, there were any number of superb Polish intelligence officers spread across Europe, whose tens of thousands of reports led to some 22,000 MI6 reports, many of them of the highest calibre and some from the unlikeliest of sources. Since the pre-war threats to Poland's integrity came not just from Germany in the west but also from the Soviet Union in the east, the Poles had set up a productive intelligence-sharing partnership with Japan, which also felt under threat from the Soviet Union. The exchange continued until the Japanese entered the war in December 1941, and at one point the Poles even had an intelligence officer in the Japanese embassy in Berlin, passing information out to Stockholm in the Japanese diplomatic bag.

The Poles had around 30 agent networks spread across occupied Europe, with several hundred agents collecting intelligence under the direction of the former MI6 station chief in Paris, Wilfred "Biffy" Dunderdale, known to the Poles as "Bifski". They included the joint Franco-Polish *Interallié* network, one of a number of networks set up in 1940 by Mieczysław Zygfryd Słowikowski (codenamed Rygor) and Wincenty Zarembski (Tudor). *Interallié*, covering much of

THE SHETLAND BUS

One of the best wartime liaison relationships between MI6 and the exiled intelligence services was with the Norwegian FOII. There was no shortage of Norwegians prepared to go back into their homeland as agents to monitor German troop movements and, more importantly, the passage of German warships into the North Sea from the Baltic and along the Norwegian coast. After the German invasion of April 1940, a regular flow of refugees arrived in Scotland and the Shetland Isles in traditional Norwegian fishing smacks, known as skøyter or puffers because of the loud popping noise made by their single-cylinder semi-diesel engines. MI6 officer Leslie Mitchell, an expert on Norway, set up a flotilla of puffers based in the Shetland port of Lerwick, which were used to ferry the agents in and out of Norway and became known as "the Shetland Bus". Mitchell operated from Flemington, a large house 16 kilometres (10 miles) west of Lerwick, where agents departing for Norway were briefed and those returning debriefed.

occupied France and Belgium, was run by Roman Garby-Czerniawski, and produced "outstanding" reports on the German order of battle in both countries. Słowikowski moved to Algiers in the spring of 1941, setting up extensive networks across North Africa which provided crucial intelligence ahead of the Allied landings there in November 1942.

The Lombard network, based in Poland itself, collected the bulk of the intelligence on the development of Germany's V1

RIGHT A remarkably accurate drawing of a V1 flying bomb, produced from intelligence largely provided by Polish agents at the test site in Germany.

and V2 rockets at Peenemünde, as well as details of German fighter aircraft, tank and submarine development. But in many ways, the leading agent was undoubtedly Halina Szymańska, the wife of the pre-war Polish military attaché in Berlin, who moved to Switzerland on the outbreak of war and was used by Admiral Wilhelm Canaris, the anti-Nazi head of the Abwehr, to feed intelligence on German plans to MI6.

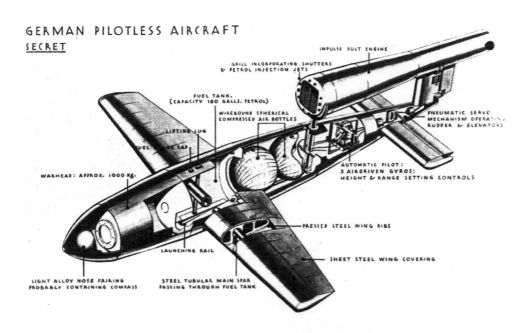

GERMAN PILOTLESS AIRCRAFT
SECRET

IMPULSE DUCT ENGINE

GRILL INCORPORATING SHUTTERS & PETROL INJECTION JETS

FUEL TANK. (CAPACITY 180 GALLS. PETROL)

WIREBOUND SPHERICAL COMPRESSED AIR BOTTLES

PNEUMATIC SERVO MECHANISM OPERATING RUDDER & ELEVATORS

LIFTING LUG

FUEL TANK CAP.

AUTOMATIC PILOT: 3 AIRDRIVEN GYROS: HEIGHT & RANGE SETTING CONTROLS

WARHEAD: APPROX. 1000 Kg.

PRESSED STEEL WING RIBS

SHEET STEEL WING COVERING

LAUNCHING RAIL

LIGHT ALLOY NOSE FAIRING PROBABLY CONTAINING COMPASS

STEEL TUBULAR MAIN SPAR PASSING THROUGH FUEL TANK

HALINA MARIA SZYMAŃSKA (1906–1989)

Halina Szymańsku, the wife of the former Polish military attaché in Berlin, was a confidante of the head of the Abwehr, Admiral Wilhelm Canaris, who opposed the Nazis and used her to pass information to the British. "He had a penchant for attractive ladies," a former MI6 officer said. "He was able to arrange for her and her children to travel in a sealed railway carriage across Germany from Poland to Switzerland, where he maintained contact with her. Indeed, he himself visited her in Berne a number of times." The product of Source Warlock, as Madame Szymańska was known, began spectacularly at the end of 1940 with a full rundown of German plans to invade Greece

via Bulgaria and Yugoslavia, which would be occupied "with or without" its government's permission, the former MI6 officer said. "The most important news reported by Szymańska was in January 1941, when she was able to tell us that an irrevocable decision had been made by Hitler to attack Russia. This valuable nugget of intelligence was passed to the Russians. Unfortunately, Stalin discounted it as misinformation." The Joint Intelligence Committee described the material coming out of the Berne station as the "most valuable and among the best reports received from any quarter". Her French identity card (left) in a false name allowed her to meet Canaris in France.

SOE OPERATIONS IN WESTERN AND CENTRAL EUROPE

Churchill's directive that the SOE should "set Europe ablaze" and the timing of its formation in July 1940 inevitably meant that its earliest and in many ways best operations took place in Western Europe, and particularly in France and Norway, where domestic resistance was at its most effective.

LEFT Henri Frager, head of the Donkeyman circuit, died in Buchenwald.

OPPOSITE The Norsk Hydro plant at Rjukan. The SOE attack on the plant was recreated in the film *The Heroes of Telemark*.

There were a number of useful operations in Denmark but resistance there was slow to get going and it was not until December 1941 that the first of around 50 SOE agents was sent in. But by the time of the Allied invasion of Europe in 1944, resistance in Denmark was strong enough to keep half a dozen German divisions tied down, providing a very useful contribution to the Allied effort. A lack of MI6 networks in Denmark meant that the SOE was also responsible for collecting intelligence there.

One of the most spectacular SOE operations was mounted in Norway where, in February 1943, the "Gunnerside" team of six SOE agents, operating under cover as students on a skiing holiday, staged an attack on the Norsk Hydro plant at Rjukan. The attack, recreated in the film *The Heroes of Telemark*, disrupted German supplies of heavy water, which could have been used in the Nazi atomic weapons research programme. All but one of the SOE agents sent into Norway were Norwegians.

SOE operations in Belgium, run at one point by the fashion designer Hardy Amies with code-names based on fashion accessories, were efficient, albeit bedevilled by arguments among Belgian politicians. In contrast, operations in the Netherlands were a disaster, with all the SOE agents rounded up by the German intelligence service, the Abwehr, in Operation Nordpol (see opposite).

The Polish Home Army provided such extensive resistance to the Nazis that there was very little for SOE to do there other than to help where they could. Around 500 successful drops of personnel and stores were made to the Home Army, but of the

more than 300 agents parachuted in, only four were British, with the remainder members of the Home Army. However, the distance to Poland took its toll, with the RAF losing 73 of the aircraft that took part in the drops.

Like those in Norway, SOE missions inside Czechoslovakia were effective, but all else was overshadowed by one single famous event, Operation Anthropoid, the assassination of Reinhard Heydrich, Governor of Bohemia and Moravia. Two Czech agents trained as assassins by the SOE ambushed and shot Heydrich on 27 May 1942. Although only wounded in the attack, he subsequently died in still unexplained circumstances (see page 55). A small number of SOE attempts to stir trouble in neighbouring Hungary failed miserably.

The most successful SOE operations capitalized on the strength of the French resistance, although initially it took time to get circuits up and running, a process that understandably met with greater success in the unoccupied Vichy-run south of the country. But by 1943, SOE had most of France covered. The networks were run via a number of different sections, the main two being RF section, which dealt with the Gaullist resistance networks, and F section, under Maurice Buckmaster,

OPERATION NORDPOL

Operation Nordpol, masterminded by Abwehr officer Major Hermann Giskes (below), was the worst failure suffered by SOE in the first part of the war. It followed the arrest in early 1942 of an SOE agent in Holland, who was forced under duress to send fake messages back to London. He omitted a security check in his messages in an attempt to alert London to the problem but this was ignored and agents continued to be sent in. A total of 53 Dutch agents were subsequently sent to Holland by SOE, most of whom were killed. This led to major recriminations from the Dutch government after the war.

which handled independent networks like the communists. The resistance relied on the SOE not just for air drops of weapons and explosives, but also for co-ordination of their activities. Tony Brooks, codenamed Alphonse, was the youngest of the SOE officers parachuted into France in 1942, aged just 20. He set up the Pimento circuit of railway workers, which attacked German troop and supply trains travelling north from Marseilles. The Pimento network's communications with F section were passed along the railway lines to Annemasse in Switzerland. Brooks split his network into small cells, ensuring that few of his men knew anyone outside their own small group and as a result, Pimento survived several minor Gestapo penetrations. Its main area of attack was the railways. It derailed numerous troop trains and, after D-Day, completely shut down the mainline railway system in southern France, preventing German reinforcements from heading north.

The biggest circuit in southern France was run by Francis Cammaerts, also working to F Section. Cammaerts, son of the Belgian poet Émile Cammaerts, had been a conscientious objector at the start of the war, but was persuaded by an old college friend, Harry Rée, to join him in SOE. Cammaerts was landed in France by an RAF Lysander light aircraft in March 1943 to join Henri Frager's Donkeyman circuit. He swiftly realized something was wrong. An Abwehr colonel who claimed to be anti-Nazi was

assisting Frager but, as the official history notes, "Cammaerts most wisely distrusted the smell of the whole affair" and cut all contacts with Donkeyman immediately. The German "colonel" turned out to be not anti-Nazi at all, but a very efficient Abwehr sergeant, Hugo Bleicher, who had successfully infiltrated the network, just one of his many successes. Shortly after Cammaerts broke off contact, Frager was arrested. Cammaerts, codenamed Roger, based himself in Provence, where he created the Jockey circuit. At its height, it had 10,000 members and its area of operations stretched from the Mediterranean to Lyons in central France and across to the Swiss and Italian borders. Security was extremely tight. Although Cammaerts knew how to get in touch with every member of his group, they could contact him only through a network of "letter-boxes" – agents who accepted or handed over a message on receipt of the correct password.

The Gaullist networks run by RF section were more difficult for SOE to control. The first and most prominent British officer sent into France by RF section was Squadron-Leader Edward Yeo-Thomas, codenamed Seahorse, who parachuted into occupied France on 25 February 1943 to help unite the various resistance movements into the Conseil National de la Résistance. But disaster struck in June 1943 when 16 Gaullist resistance members were arrested at Caluire, near Lyons. Yeo-Thomas returned to France twice to

FAR LEFT Edward Yeo-Thomas, "the white rabbit", who persuaded Churchill to give the French resistance more supplies and was tortured by the Gestapo.

LEFT Francis Cammaerts, one of the most successful of the SOE officers operating with the French resistance.

ABOVE The French communist Maquis were dismissed as irrelevant by SOE until they destroyed the Bussy-Varache Viaduct in March 1943.

deal with the aftermath of the arrests, but the second time, in February 1944, was himself arrested. Despite repeated beatings and torture by the Gestapo, he refused to talk. After several attempts to get free, he was taken to Buchenwald, from where he did successfully escape. Recaptured and taken to a prisoner-of-war camp near Marienburg, he again escaped and made his way back across Allied lines. His exploits earned him the George Cross and the nickname "the White Rabbit".

OPERATION ANTHROPOID

Reinhard Heydrich, the head of the *Reichsicherheitshauptamt*, was appointed acting governor of the Czech provinces of Bohemia and Moravia in September 1941. This left him vulnerable to an assassination attempt and SOE sent two Czech agents, Jozef Gabčík and Jan Kubiš, to kill him. They ambushed Heydrich's car on 27 May 1942 injuring him with an anti-personnel grenade. Heydrich fought back and the assassination attempt appeared to have failed, but he died in hospital a week later, apparently of blood poisoning. Anomalies in Heydrich's condition and modifications to the grenade have led to suspicions that it contained a bacteriological agent.

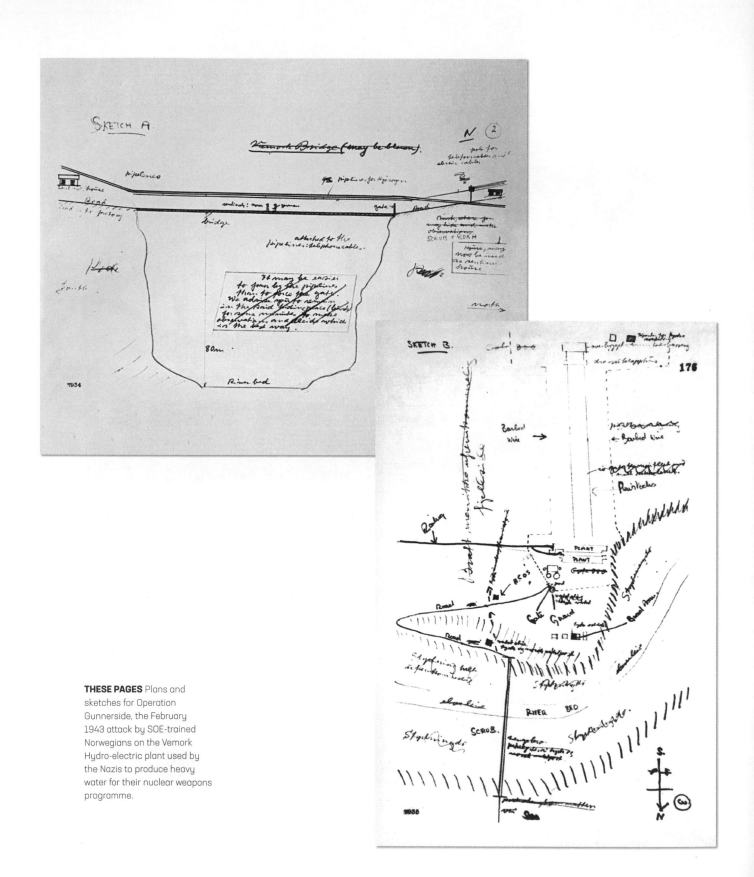

THESE PAGES Plans and sketches for Operation Gunnerside, the February 1943 attack by SOE-trained Norwegians on the Vemork Hydro-electric plant used by the Nazis to produce heavy water for their nuclear weapons programme.

30.   Especial care will be taken to avoid farms where children are seen, or where there is a telephone.

31.   No use will be made of public transport.

<u>Distribution</u>

Copy No. 1   Force Commander
             (CD(0)
             Royal Norwegian High Command
             File

Copy No. 2   Operation Instruction No 1.

15th December, 1942.

MOST SECRET   159

GUNNERSIDE

<u>INFORMATION</u>

<u>Technical</u>

1.   The enemy is utilising the power available at VEMORK 59° 55' N. 08° 29' E. for large scale experiments of a highly secret nature which it is judged essential to bring to a standstill.   This entails the destruction of the finishing stages of production.

<u>Enemy</u>

2.   RJUKAN   Enemy strength now over 100, consisting largely of Gestapo

3.   MOESHAMMEN   40 Germans, probably A.A. crews of 4 A.A. guns 20mm at dam.

4.   VEMORK   Some Gestapo still present.   Guard of 1 N.C.O. and 12 men.   Searchlight on roof of target building. Machine gun also reported in same position.   Both believed to be directed on pipe-line.

5.   <u>Along Withdrawal Route</u>   Enemy posts to be expected after attack at all bridges over main valley crossings, and in fair mobile strength in the valleys.

6.   <u>At Frontier</u>   Any serious concentration of German guards in the frontier area unlikely.

<u>Own Troops</u>

7.   Three officers and three other ranks will comprise the main attacking force, supported by the advance party of two officers and two other ranks.

<u>INTENTION</u>

8.   Gunnerside force will attack the storage and producing plant at VEMORK with high explosive, so that present stocks and fluid in the course of production are destroyed.

<u>METHOD</u>

9.   Gunnerside force will be dropped by parachute in British uniform at a point 60° 01' N. 08° 08' E, where they will be met by the advance party.

10.   Latest tactical information will be given to Gunnerside leader by the reception party leader, and the route for the advance to the target laid down.

11.   Dumps of stores will be made for use during withdrawal.

12.   The combined party will advance to a forward base within easy reach of the target, and a final reconnaissance will be made.

INTELLIGENCE IN OCCUPIED EUROPE

MI6 lost its stations in Berlin, Vienna and Prague on the outbreak of war, but managed to retain contact with some of its agents in Germany via stations in Oslo, Stockholm and Geneva.

Nevertheless, the death of Sir Hugh Sinclair from cancer in November 1939 and the disaster of the Venlo Incident, which was unfolding even as he died, led to a series of arguments not just over his successor, but over the effectiveness of MI6 generally; the Royal Navy, the Army and the RAF all complained that they were not receiving the intelligence they needed. The appointment of Colonel Stewart Menzies as C, largely on Sinclair's recommendation, was followed by an inquiry under Lord Hankey into the secret services, which in essence cleared MI6 of many of the charges against it.

Meanwhile, working on the back of information supplied by the Polish codebreakers, Bletchley Park had begun to make inroads into the German Enigma cipher, using material intercepted by wireless operators in stations around the UK. Hut 6, the Enigma codebreaking section working on German army and air force Enigma material, began to enjoy limited success. When the Germans invaded Norway in April 1940, the welter of traffic that ensued allowed the codebreakers to break what they called the Yellow Enigma cipher – sadly only in use in Norway – very quickly. But it was the Battle of France, in

RIGHT Royal Navy motor torpedo boats which transported MI6 and SOE agents across the Channel to France.

BELOW When Germany invaded France, Breton fishermen fled across the Channel to Cornwall. Based at Helford, they ferried MI6 agents to France.

THE OSLO REPORT

The Oslo Report was posted to the British embassy in Oslo in November 1939. It included details of the latest Nazi scientific developments, including two types of radar and the V1 flying bombs, as well as an actual electronic proximity fuse far better than anything the British had. It was sent by Hans Ferdinand Mayer, a German scientist (right). A Jewish friend of Mayer had been helped out of Germany by Frank Foley, the pre-war MI6 station chief in Berlin. The grateful Mayer was told to send any intelligence he had to the Oslo embassy because Foley was to be based there at the start of the war.

which large numbers of troops took part, which allowed Hut 6 to break into the Red Enigma cipher used by Luftwaffe officers liaising with the ground forces. "The Red" was to become the most productive of all the Enigma ciphers, providing details of German plans and operations across Europe, which were sent on to the three services disguised at MI6 agent reports to ensure as few people as possible knew that Bletchley had cracked the supposedly unbreakable Enigma ciphers.

Although it is still widely believed that MI6 had lost all its networks in occupied Europe when the Germans invaded, in fact there were a number of agents inside Germany being run from Stockholm and Sweden, as well as intelligence from Polish, Norwegian and Czech agents supplied by the Allied governments-in-exile in London. Despite complaints from the navy, there was in fact a well-established MI6 ship-watching service in place, with reports coming from agents in Norway, Sweden, Denmark, the Baltic republics and even Kiel inside Germany itself. But the loss of stations across occupied Europe forced MI6 to focus on obtaining intelligence via the stations it retained in the neutral capitals of Madrid, Lisbon, Geneva and Stockholm.

Some of the British agents inside Germany were foreign workers; others were trade unionists. MI6 appears to have taken over links to the International Transport Federation set up by naval intelligence before the war, collecting large amounts of information, including details of German weapons production.

RIGHT Paul Rosbaud, who kept the British informed throughout the war on the lack of progress of the German atomic weapons programme.

One Norwegian agent run by the MI6 station in Stockholm had such good contacts in Germany that he was given access to its military facilities. Among the intelligence he supplied was the crucial report that the *Bismarck* was leaving the Baltic, allowing the Royal Navy to hunt her down in May 1941.

Meanwhile, the introduction from August 1940 of large numbers of electro-mechanical devices known as Bombes to try out potential plain text hidden in the Enigma messages dramatically increased the amount of intelligence being produced by Bletchley Park, which grew to a level where it became impossible to disguise it all as agent reports. Very few of the large number of the many different Enigma ciphers introduced by the Germans evaded the British codebreakers. They were thus able to provide extensive intelligence on German activities all over occupied Europe. Special liaison units run by MI6 were set up to distribute the Bletchley Park reports, but only very few senior officers were told where the intelligence came from, which had the welcome side effect for MI6 of improving its own reputation.

Thanks largely to Foley's pre-war efforts, MI6 had a number of key agents inside Germany, including Paul Rosbaud, whose Jewish wife had been helped to escape from pre-war Berlin by Foley, earning her husband's gratitude. Rosbaud was close to a number of leading German scientists and as scientific advisor to the Springer Verlag publishing house, was kept abreast of all the latest scientific developments in Germany. His reports were written in secret ink and hidden under letters to his wife which were sent via Sweden. He also provided intelligence on the German rocket experiments at Peenemünde and assisted a young Norwegian agent, Sverre Bergh, sent in by MI6 to gather more details from the test site itself. But the most important

THE HELFORD FISHING FLEET

The problem of inserting agents into France was solved separately by SOE and MI6 through the creation of private fleets of Breton fishing boats which had moved to Cornwall and fast motor torpedo boats. MI6 initially ran its fishing smacks out of Mylor Creek, three kilometres (two miles) north of Falmouth, while its motor torpedo boats were based in Dover, Portsmouth and Dartmouth, and agents were also taken to France by submarine. SOE set up base in Helford, eight kilometres (five miles) southwest of Falmouth. Eventually, the two operations were combined at Helford under the control of Commander Frank Slocum, a senior MI6 officer.

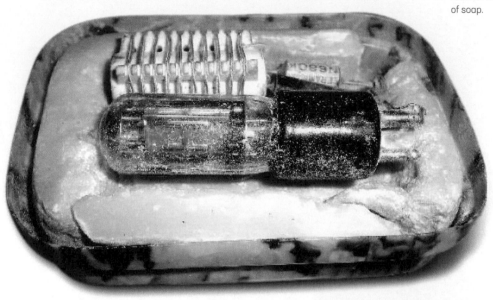

LEFT A small agent wireless receiver hidden inside a bar of soap.

intelligence that Rosbaud reported was the lack of German progress in the attempt to produce atomic weapons.

The Stockholm station also ran a number of intelligence networks in Berlin, Hamburg, Bonn, Königsberg and Vienna. The most extensive description available of these networks comes from the German interrogation of MI6 agent R34. Carl Aage Andreasson, a Danish businessman who was able to travel in and out of Germany, was captured by German intelligence in January 1944. He told his interrogators that there were four separate British networks in Berlin alone, while in Hamburg there were 80 agents working for the British. Andreasson, known as Source Elgar, smuggled microfilmed reports out in crates of goods exported to Sweden. His sub-agents included technical workers at Peenemünde and an employee at the Berlin office of a company manufacturing Messerschmitt aircraft in Hungary. Another agent, Outcast, run from Finland by Harry Carr, provided extensive intelligence from inside Germany, including good reports on damage done to Berlin by RAF

bombing raids. He was described in a post-war report as "one of the most successful spies against Germany that the 1939–45 war produced", which, given the success of spies like Rosbaud and Andreasson, was praise indeed.

Apart from the large amount of intelligence MI6 was collecting from inside Germany itself, the networks in France were also important producers of intelligence, mainly naval and military. Some of the French networks were controlled by the Gaullist Bureau Central de Renseignements et d'Action, others by the Poles, while some of the Free French networks, like the large Davis and Alliance networks, were run directly by MI6. Alongside reports on the dislocation of German troops in France, they provided extensive details of German naval movements. All of the U-boat ports on the French Atlantic coast were covered extensively and the networks also provided vital intelligence for the 1942 commando raids on Dieppe and Saint-Nazaire. The most important intelligence they provided was for D-Day.

PW/A

1B

RECOMMENDATION FOR MILITARY AWARD.

a) Name   KEUN, Gerald George Philip

   Nationality   Dutch

   Rank   Held the rank of Captain in the
                                           British Army in the name of KANE,
                                           Gerald George Philip

b) Award for which recommended: George Cross (Posthumous)

c) Status   Officer in the British Army

d) CITATION

KEUN started working for the British Intelligence in France at the end of 1941. By the middle of 1942 his contacts had so far developed that he moved to Paris, where he set up his own organisation with direct communications with London.

During the following twelve months KEUN made two return visits to the U.K., once by air operation and once by sea. Subsidiary sections of his organisation were established in Lyons, Bordeaux, the Loire region and the north of France. For six months of this period, he was also in charge of a pick-up operations group, which maintained a monthly courier service with London.

Two days after he arrived in this country for the second time, KEUN learned by telegram that his co-chief in France had been seriously wounded by the Gestapo and had been forced into hiding. Fearing that the flow of information to England would suffer as a result of this accident, and in spite of very real physical fatigue after his journey to the U.K., KEUN insisted on returning to France immediately. His parachute landing, however, was not successful, and his spinal vertebrae were severely injured. In spite of his doctor's advice that unless he remained on his back for some months he would be crippled for life, on at least three occasions he discarded his plaster cast, and in spite of great suffering cycled seventy miles to ensure the delivery of a courier to an agent due to leave for England.

KEUN was arrested by the Gestapo on 29th June, 1944, was deported to Germany and was hanged at Buchenwald on 9th September, 1944.

Throughout his service, KEUN showed the highest possible courage and devotion to duty. His personal example was an inspiration to those who followed him, and his accomplishments in the field contributed largely to the liberation of France.

K/Comm
27-8-47

A 9082   P.T.O.

THE HESS "STING"

Rudolf Hess, Hitler's deputy, flew to Britain in May 1941 intent on brokering a peace deal with Britain.

Hitler was about to turn on his Soviet ally and a number of senior Nazis, including Hess, believed that members of the British establishment who had expressed admiration for Hitler before the war would be willing to negotiate a peace with Germany in order to fight communism. Controversy has raged ever since over the true nature of Hess's mission, with a number of books suggesting that he was lured to Britain in a sting operation carried out by British intelligence. The truth is naturally more arcane than the conspiracy theories, but does explain how the idea that Hess was lured to the United Kingdom took hold.

Hess's foreign affairs adviser was Albrecht Haushofer, a close friend of the Duke of Hamilton. Before the war the Duke had been a member of the Anglo-German Fellowship, a right-wing group dedicated to closer relations between Britain and the Third Reich. Haushofer's parents were in contact with an English friend, a Mrs Violet Roberts, exchanging harmless letters via a box number at the Thomas Cook office in Lisbon.

Haushofer agreed to send a letter to Hamilton, via Mrs Roberts, suggesting they meet in Lisbon. The letter, sent on 23 September 1940, suggested Hamilton, and his "friends in high places", might "find some significance" in Haushofer's offer of such a meeting and gave him an address in Lisbon to which he should send his response, placing it in an envelope marked "Dr A H, nothing more!", which should be put in a second envelope addressed to Minero Silricola Ltd, Rua do Cais de Santarem 32/1, Lisbon, Portugal.

ABOVE Albrecht Haushofer (left), Hess's foreign policy adviser, talking to the Swedish explorer Sven Hedin in Berlin in 1935.

OPPOSITE Rudolf Hess, Hitler's deputy, sincerely believed that Britain and Germany could make peace to fight the common enemy, the Soviet Union.

The letter was intercepted by MI5, which initially suspected that Hamilton and Roberts might be part of a German spy ring. Haushofer had visited the United Kingdom before the war and was thought to be a German spy. But it took only a few weeks to realize that the letter was a genuine attempt to seek peace. It was only then that MI6 was informed. There was discussion over whether or not it might be possible to use Haushofer to

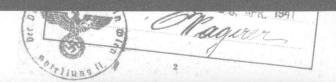

64

ABOVE The city of Lisbon, to which MI6 planned to entice Hess or Haushofer until it was deemed it too risky. MI5 had separate but similar plans, which were also dropped.

obtain intelligence on German intentions and to feed false information back to the Nazis. MI5 remained uncertain how to respond, but Stewart Menzies, the head of MI6, believed it was a rare opportunity to gather intelligence on the Nazi regime. The head of the MI6 station in Lisbon was asked to investigate the company and reported back that it was "well known as a German-controlled corporation".

Menzies decided to explore the possibility of a sting operation to gather evidence on Nazi plans for the invasions of the United

Kingdom and the Soviet Union, and to create splits in the German camp. He kept his plans from MI5 but, conscious of how MI6 had itself been stung in the Venlo incident, he sent Frank Foley, the pre-war head of station in Berlin, to Lisbon to evaluate whether the sting was feasible or sensible. Foley was head of A1, the MI6 German section, and the most experienced German specialist in MI6; he was the obvious person to determine whether or not the operation might work.

The diary of Foley's wife, Kay, records that he flew to Lisbon on Friday 17 January 1941, accompanied by his assistant Margaret Reid. Quite how they tested the feasibility of the sting operation remains the only real remaining mystery in the Hess story. The one effective way of checking it out was to respond

to the letter and to arrange to meet either Haushofer or another intermediary in the Portuguese capital. Whatever Foley and Reid did in Lisbon, it took a full two weeks. They arrived back in England on 1 February 1941 with bad news. The sting was too risky. The idea was abandoned.

MI5 had no idea that MI6 was investigating the possibility of mounting a sting operation, but while Foley was in Portugal, it decided on a completely separate, albeit somewhat similar, course of action. Three days after Foley flew to Lisbon, Dick White, John Masterman and Tommy "Tar" Robertson, MI5's leading experts on German espionage operations against Britain, met to discuss the letter. Like Menzies, they decided they wanted to know more about Haushofer's motivation and whether or not he was putting forward a genuine attempt to achieve peace. They decided Hamilton should be informed of the letter and should be told that "he might be of considerable assistance to the country if he paid a visit to Lisbon, got into touch with Haushofer and discovered what was at the back of his mind".

But there were severe doubts over the feasibility of using Hamilton and it was not until well over a month later that the letter's existence was revealed to him and he was questioned about his relationship with Haushofer. Several weeks later, on 25 March 1941, he was interviewed by "Tar" Robertson, who asked him whether he was happy to go to Lisbon to meet Haushofer. He was not expected to do anything difficult, Robertson said. All he had to do was to listen to what Haushofer had to say and report it back to MI5. Hamilton agreed to go to Lisbon under certain conditions, but still the affair dragged on.

Meanwhile, Hess, frustrated over the apparent failure to make contact via Hamilton and intent on speaking to the Duke in person, flew to Britain on 10 May 1941 in a Luftwaffe Messerschmitt-110. He bailed out shortly before his aircraft crashed south of Glasgow. It was only the next day, 11 May 1941, that MI5 finally decided to abandon the idea of getting Haushofer and Hamilton together in Lisbon.

Hess was held in Mytchett Place near Aldershot in Hampshire, where every conversation he had was recorded via hidden microphones. A number of British officials still believed there must be a way of using him to aid the war effort. Foley interviewed him several times, but eventually decided he was mad and there was no way in which he could be useful. Hess was held at a military hospital in Abergavenny in Wales until the end of the war, when he was put on trial at Nuremberg as a war criminal. He was sentenced to life imprisonment and remained in Spandau jail in Berlin until his death in 1987.

FOLEY AND THE JEWS

Frank Foley was the MI6 head of station in Berlin from 1921 to shortly before the war in August 1939. A devout Roman Catholic, he was deeply antagonistic towards the Nazis. His cover was as head of the British Passport Control Office, which provided visas not just for Britain and the Empire but also for Palestine, which Britain administered under mandate from the League of Nations. Inundated with requests from frightened Jews wishing to travel to Palestine, Foley twisted the rules on who could have visas in order to help them leave. He went into the concentration camps to get Jews out, provided them with visas and in some cases false passports, and hid them in his own home. All this despite the fact that he had no diplomatic immunity and that the Germans, who were aware he was a spy, might arrest him at any time. Benno Cohn, president of the German Zionist Organization, told the 1961 trial of Adolf Eichmann that Foley was the "Pimpernel of the Jews" and had rescued "thousands of Jews from the jaws of death". On 25 February 1999, Yad Vashem, Israel's Holocaust Memorial Centre, named him Righteous Among the Nations, the highest award the Jewish people can grant to a gentile.

RIGHT AND FOLLOWING PAGES The letter from Albrecht Haushofer, an adviser to Deputy Führer Rudolf Hess, to his friend the Duke of Hamilton, proposing a meeting in Lisbon to discuss peace talks between Hess and Hamilton's "friends in high places".

OPPOSITE The wreckage of Hess's Messerschmidt-110, which crashed after he bailed out over Scotland on his ill-conceived mission to the UK.

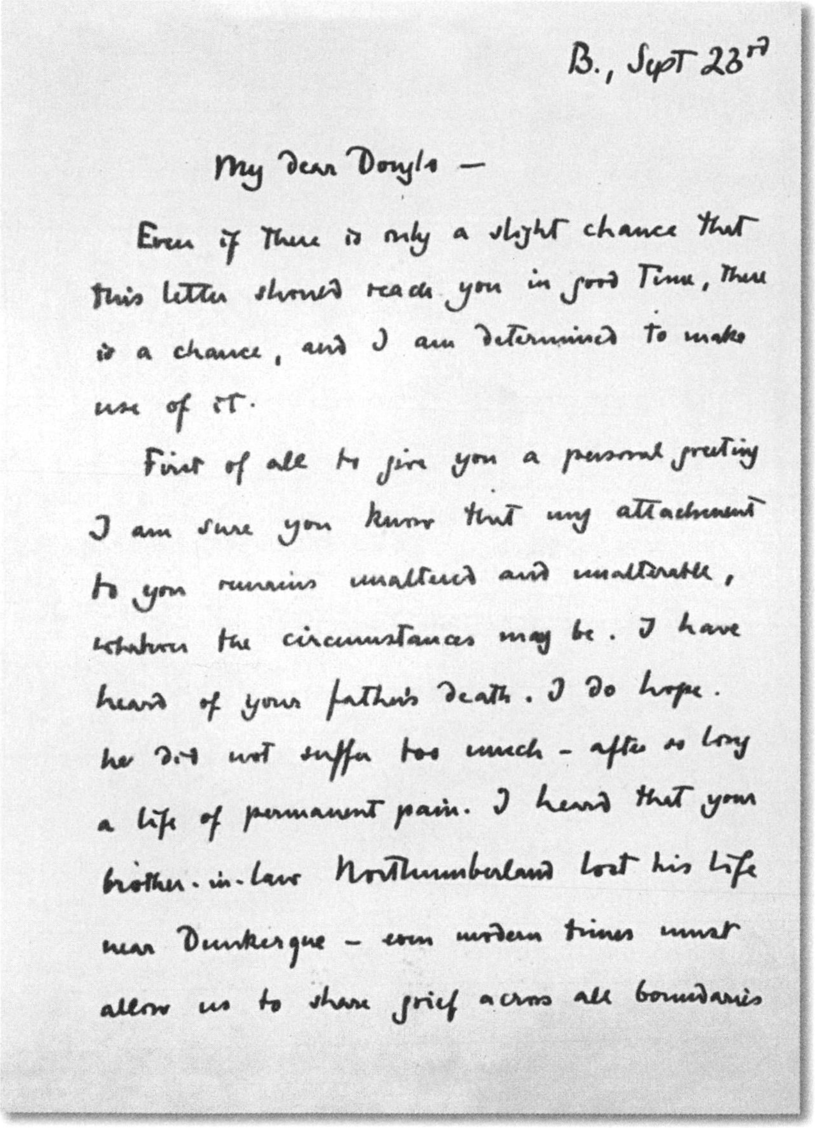

B., Sept 23rd

My dear Douglo —

Even if there is only a slight chance that this letter should reach you in good time, there is a chance, and I am determined to make use of it.

First of all to give you a personal greeting. I am sure you know that my attachment to you remains unaltered and unalterable, whatever the circumstances may be. I have heard of your father's death. I do hope he did not suffer too much – after so long a life of permanent pain. I heard that your brother-in-law Northumberland lost his life near Dunkerque – even modern times must allow us to share grief across all boundaries

But it is not only the story of death
that should find its place in this letter.
If you remember some of my last communications in July 1939 you may find some
— and your friends in high places —
significance in the fact that I am able
to ask you whether you could find time
to have a talk with me somewhere on
the outskirts of ~~the~~ Europe, perhaps in
Portugal. I could reach Lisbon any . .
time (and without any kind of difficulties)
within a few days after receiving news
from you. Of course I do not know whether
you can make your authorities understand
so much, that they give you leave ...

But at least you may be able to answer my question. Letters will reach me (fairly quickly ; they would take some four or five days from Lisbon on the utmost) in the following way : Double closed envelope . Inside adress : „Dr. A.H.ʺ nothing more ! Outside adress

„ Minero Silvicola Ltd.
            Rua do Cais de Santarem 32/$\underline{I}$
                    Lisbon . Portugal ʺ

My father and mother add their wishes for your personal welfare to my own ....

        Yours ever

            A.

INTELLIGENCE IN NORTH AFRICA

The first British military ground campaign in which the intelligence produced as a result of the breaking of the German Enigma ciphers at Bletchley Park made a significant difference was that in North Africa.

The success against a number of Enigma ciphers used by German forces there led the codebreakers to set up an outpost in Cairo in November 1940 to disseminate the Enigma intelligence, now codenamed Ultra. The codebreakers and intelligence reporters working at the Combined Bureau Middle East, based in the former Flora and Fauna Museum in Heliopolis, were linked to Bletchley by a Special Signals Link.

MI6 had also set up a regional headquarters in Cairo to cover the Middle East, North Africa and the Balkans, which operated under the cover name of the Inter-Services Liaison Department. This was run by Captain Cuthbert Bowlby, a Royal Navy officer, who during the first half of 1941 had a very good network operating in Tunisia under cover of the Société d'Étude et des Pêcheries run by André Mounier, a French lawyer. The network's young members were carelessly over-enthusiastic and as a result it was soon rolled up by the Germans. Other MI6 agents were inserted into Libya and Tunisia by the Long-Range Desert Group, a British Army special forces reconnaissance unit set up in June 1940 to operate behind enemy lines in North Africa.

By now, large numbers of different Enigma systems were in use by German ground forces and the Luftwaffe units that were supporting them, which, together with the breaking of the Italian C38m machine cipher in June 1941, allowed the codebreakers to produce precise details of the routes of the Mediterranean naval convoys taking supplies to the German troops. In order to protect the Ultra secret, the ships had to be "spotted" by RAF reconnaissance aircraft before they could be attacked and sunk, but the codebreakers' intelligence ensured that the RAF and the Royal Navy were soon cutting a swathe through the German supply lines. This was one of the first instances where Bletchley Park had a major impact on the war in North Africa, but it was not the only one.

In August 1942, with a seemingly unstoppable Afrika Korps advancing on Cairo, the German commander Field Marshal Erwin Rommel discussed his plans with Hitler over a link using the Red Enigma cipher. An MI6 Special Liaison Unit set up to pass on the top-secret Ultra material to the new commander of the British Eighth Army, General Bernard Montgomery, informed him that the deciphered messages showed that Rommel planned to attack through the Alam Halfa ridge and encircle the Eighth Army. Bletchley's confirmation of Rommel's plans allowed Montgomery to block the German advance and set up the decisive battle at El Alamein, which began on 23 October 1942. By now Bletchley's intelligence was ensuring that only half of Rommel's supplies were getting through, crippling his campaign. So tight were his margins of supply that the sinking of a single convoy during the battle itself had a direct influence on the fighting.

On the afternoon of 2 November, with Montgomery about to deliver the killer blow, Bletchley deciphered a message from Rommel to Hitler asking permission to withdraw. "*Panzerarmee ist erschopft*," he said, "The Panzer Army is exhausted." The response from Hitler was that Rommel should stand his ground at all costs. He was to "show no other road to his troops than the road leading to death or victory". Two days later the battle was over and the Afrika Korps was in retreat.

Although the codebreakers' intelligence played no major part in the El Alamein victory, they were able to provide details of the state of Rommel's forces both before the battle and in its immediate aftermath, revealing that the "Desert Fox" had virtually no fuel and only 11 serviceable tanks left. The codebreakers were furious that the cautious Montgomery did not use the intelligence to finish Rommel off, but from then on, as the Eighth Army advanced across North Africa, the Bletchley Park intelligence played a vital role in Montgomery's decision-making.

ABOVE The British Eighth Army was reinforced with the very fast but under-gunned Crusader tank. Montgomery had more than 200 Crusader IIs at el Alamein.

RIGHT General Bernard Montgomery in North Africa. He benefited from Bletchley Park intelligence but did not to use it to the full against Rommel.

Within days of the British victory at El Alamein, Allied forces landed in Morocco, Algeria and Tunisia as part of Operation Torch, the invasion of North Africa, an operation designed to provide a base from which to attack Italy and southern France. MI6 was able to provide superb intelligence on the situation across the region. This was largely provided by Mieczysław Zygfryd Słowikowski, a Polish intelligence officer known by the codename Rygor. Słowikowski ran the Polish intelligence networks in North Africa under the guise of his position as owner of a factory producing breakfast cereal. His Station Africa network had bases in Algiers, Oran, Tunis, Casablanca and Dakar, providing detailed information on German and Vichy French military capabilities and defences, which was passed back to MI6 in London and direct to the Americans via the US Consul-General in Algiers, Robert Daniel Murphy.

Operation Torch saw US and British troops, under the command of US General Dwight Eisenhower, occupy French North Africa and push east with the aim of linking up with Montgomery. German commanders began pouring troops into Tunis, a reinforcement chronicled in some detail by Bletchley. An Egyptian Jew, known as Dick Jones, originally sent in to Tunisia by MI6 in September 1941 to set up a network there but captured before he could do anything, was released and began operating immediately, using agents recruited from fellow prisoners also now free. Over the next four months, as the Germans fought vainly against the US-led troops advancing from the west and the Eighth Army attacking from Libya in the east, the Jones network was just one of a number providing critical intelligence on German military activities in Tunisia, an effort which restored MI6's reputation. Jones was finally captured by the Gestapo in February 1943 but managed to persuade the Germans he was a British officer and ended up in Colditz, the castle in southern Germany used to hold Allied prisoners of war who refused to stop trying to escape.

By now, Allied troops were closing in on Rommel. In a last-ditch attempt to destroy the British Eighth Army and enable himself to hold off the Allied forces in the west, the Desert Fox prepared to throw three of his Panzer divisions against Montgomery. But Ultra ensured the British general knew every detail of the German plans. When Rommel's 160 tanks attacked the Eighth Army positions at Medenine on the morning of 6 March, they were faced by a solid wall of 470 anti-tank guns, 350 field guns and 400 tanks. Fed by the codebreakers with every detail of his planned assault, the British simply sat and waited for him. By evening, his forces largely destroyed, Rommel called off the battle. Three days later he left Africa, never to return.

ABOVE Mieczyslaw Slowikowski, codename Rygor, set up an agent network based in Algiers for the Torch landings.

OPPOSITE Field Marshal Erwin Rommel in North Africa three months after El Alamein, having replenished his supplies of tanks.

OPERATION MINCEMEAT

The body of a dead tramp was used in an ingenious plan to deceive the Germans into believing that Allied forces would invade southern Europe via Sardinia and Greece. The real invasion was to start with an attack on Sicily in July 1943 and then move up Italy. The body of Glyndwr Michael was dressed in the uniform of a Royal Marine officer (below) and dropped from an aircraft off Spain as if he had been

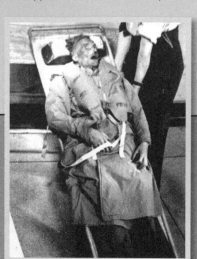

in an aircraft that crashed. "Major William Martin" had a courier's briefcase chained to his wrist. It contained documents and letters between British generals, one of which discussed planned assaults on Sardinia and Greece, while another referred jocularly to sardines, in order to reinforce the impression that the attack would come via Sardinia. Martin's persona was carefully constructed, with love letters, a photograph of his girlfriend, a bus ticket and even a letter from his bank manager demanding repayment of an overdraft placed in his pockets. The Spanish passed the documents on to the Germans and when Bletchley Park picked up messages showing that they had fallen for the ruse, a message was sent to Churchill, who was then visiting the United States, informing him "Mincemeat swallowed whole".

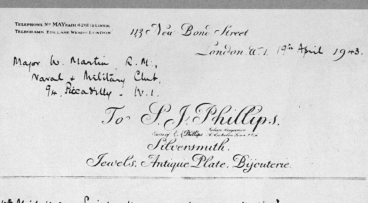

THESE PAGES AND FOLLOWING PAGES

The various documents prepared to make the dead courier in Operation Mincemeat appear to be a genuine Royal Marines officer, Major William Martin, included a letter from his bank demanding repayment of his overdraft, a photograph of his fiancée Pam and a receipt for a ring bought for her, a love letter from Pam and a letter from Lord Louis Mountbatten to Admiral Sir Andrew Cunningham, the Admiral of the Fleet, hinting with a reference to "sardines" that Sardinia was to be the site of the Allied landings in southern Europe rather than Sicily.

TELEGRAPHIC ADDRESS,
"BRANCHAGE, STOCK, LONDON."
TELEPHONE N°
MANSION HOUSE 1500.

Lloyds Bank Limited.
HEAD OFFICE,
LONDON, E.C.3.

POSTAL ADDRESS,
G.P.O. BOX 215,
71, LOMBARD STREET, E.C.3.

IN REPLYING PLEASE ADDRESS
THE JOINT GENERAL MANAGERS.

14th April, 1943.

PRIVATE.

Major W. Martin, R.M.,
    Army and Navy Club,
        Pall Mall,
            LONDON, S.W.1.

Dear Sir,

I am given to understand that in spite of repeated application your overdraft amounting to £79.19s.2d. still outstands.

In the circumstances, I am now writing to inform you that unless this amount, plus interest at 4% to date of payment, is received forthwith we shall have no alternative but to take the necessary steps to protect our interests.

Yours faithfully,

Joint General Manager.

**THE MANOR HOUSE
OGBOURNE ST. GEORGE
MARLBOROUGH
WILTSHIRE**
TELEPHONE OGBOURNE ST GEORGE 242
Sunday 18th.

I do think dearest that seeing people like you off at railway stations is one of the poorer forms of sport. I think going off can leave a howling great gap in ones life & one has to try madly — & quite in vain — to fill it with all the things one used to enjoy a whole two weeks ago. That lovely golden day we spent together — oh. I know its been said before, but if only time would sometimes stand still just for a minute — But that line of thought is too pointless. Pull your socks up Pam & dont be a silly little fool.

Your letter made me feel slightly better — but I shall get horribly conceited if you go on saying things like that about me — they're utterly unlike ME, as I'm afraid you'll soon find out. Meis. I am the big loser-end in this divine place with Mummy & Dads being too sweet & understanding this whole time, bored beyond words & waiting for Monday so that I can get back to this old civilisation again. What an idiotic oasis!

Bill darling, do let me know as soon as you get there & I can make some more plans, & dont please let them send you off into the blue the horrible way they do now a days — now that we've found each other out of this whole world. dont think I could bear it —

All my love.
Pam

Telephone :
WHitehall 9777

in reply, quote S.R.1924/43.

COMBINED OPERATIONS HEADQUARTERS,
1A, RICHMOND TERRACE,
WHITEHALL S.W.1.

21st April,
1 9 4 3.

Dear Admiral of the Fleet,

I promised V.C.I.G.S. that Major Martin would
arrange with you for the onward transmission of a
letter he has with him for General Alexander. It is
very urgent and very "hot" and as there are some
remarks in it that could not be seen by others in the
War Office, it could not go by signal. I feel sure
that you will see that it goes on safely and without
delay.

I think you will find Martin the man you want.
He is quiet and shy at first, but he really knows his
stuff. He was more accurate than some of us about the
probable run of events at Dieppe and he has been well
in on the experiments with the latest barges and
equipment which took place up in Scotland.

Let me have him back, please, as soon as the
assault is over. He might bring some sardines with him -
they are "on points" here!

Yours sincerely

Louis Mountbatten

Admiral of the Fleet Sir A.B. Cunningham, G.C.B.,D.S.O.,
Commander in Chief Mediterranean,
Allied Force H.Q.,
Algiers.

CHURCHILL'S OBSESSION WITH INTELLIGENCE

Churchill was an avid reader of intelligence. As First Lord of the Admiralty during the early stages of the First World War, he had set up the highly successful Royal Navy codebreaking operation known as Room 40 "in order to penetrate the German mind and movements and make reports".

During his time out of government from 1929 to 1939, the so-called "Wilderness Years", he was fortunate to be a friend and near neighbour of Desmond Morton, initially the head of MI6 intelligence production and later in charge of the government's industrial intelligence centre, in which role he was still a recipient of MI6 material on Nazi Germany. Morton allegedly passed Churchill secret intelligence, although evidence has been found that this was done with the authorization of government ministers. Churchill used this intelligence in his attacks on the appeasement policies pursued by Neville Chamberlain (British Prime Minister from May 1937 onwards). The relationship with Morton continued after Churchill's re-appointment as First Lord of the Admiralty on the outbreak of the Second World War, when he formed his own links with Stewart Menzies, the chief of MI6, and headed off an attempt by the Royal Navy to set up its own secret service.

By the time that Churchill became prime minister in May 1940, following the resignation of Chamberlain, the codebreakers at Bletchley Park were producing extensive intelligence on the German invasion of Norway. This was the first point at which large amounts of Enigma messages could be deciphered, although they were enciphered using a unique Enigma only used in Norway and therefore of no use elsewhere. Within days of Churchill's appointment as prime minister, the Bletchley Park codebreakers had broken the "Red" Enigma cipher, which produced the best intelligence on what German troops were doing, or planned to do, and was to become the most important Enigma cipher for Bletchley throughout the war.

Churchill swiftly appointed Morton as his personal adviser on intelligence matters, using him in the early moves to take special operations away from MI6 and create the Special Operations Executive, an ambition that was not shared either by Morton or by his friends in MI6. The new prime minister initially received much of his intelligence through Morton, but the importance of the Ultra material from Bletchley Park meant that Menzies was soon briefing Churchill on a frequent and possibly daily basis on the most important intelligence from both human agents and

OPPOSITE The Prime Minister was fascinated by intelligence and involved himself heavily in the work of both MI6 and Bletchley Park.

BELOW Churchill insisted the codebreakers should have everything they needed in a memo marked "Action This Day".

ACTION THIS DAY

IMMEDIATE

Bletchley, and providing him with copies of the actual reports when it was thought this would reinforce their importance in Churchill's mind.

The decision to provide Churchill with actual copies of the Enigma reports came from the prime minister himself, in a message relayed to Menzies by Morton, who added that Churchill had ordered that they should be sent in a locked box that was to be clearly marked: "This box is only to be opened by the Prime Minister in person." In practice, the Enigma reports provided to Churchill were only a limited number of those produced by Bletchley, but Menzies took full advantage of the opportunity to ensure that his own influence with Churchill and the reputation of both MI6 and Bletchley were enhanced, usually delivering the box personally and briefing the prime minister on intelligence matters generally.

Nor was Britain's wartime prime minister simply a passive reader of the intelligence. He was very happy to point important intelligence out to senior commanders in the field. In August 1941, amid a series of distressing reports on the mass murder of Jews as the Nazis advanced across Eastern Europe, Churchill made one of his most famous speeches, risking the Enigma secret to denounce the killings (see opposite). Following the Allied victory at El Alamein in November 1942, he bombarded General Harold Alexander, the British commander-in-chief in the Middle East, with deciphered Enigma reports showing that Rommel's forces were "in great anxiety and disarray" and urging that Alexander order Montgomery to finish off the Afrika Korps.

COVENTRY CONSPIRACY THEORY

An ongoing accusation against Winston Churchill is that he allowed the bombing raid that devastated the city of Coventry on 14 November 1940 to go ahead in order to protect the secret that Enigma had been broken. This is not true. Hut 6 was breaking what they called the Brown Enigma cipher, which revealed planned Luftwaffe targets, and this was being used to alert the RAF fighters that would intercept the bombers. But Keith Batey, one of the Hut 6 codebreakers who worked on the Brown cipher, recalled that for several days before the Coventry raid, they were unable to break it.

LEFT Desmond Morton fed Churchill intelligence before the war and was his main liaison with MI6 and Bletchley during the war.

Churchill was in no doubt as to the importance of the work at Bletchley, lauding the codebreakers later as "the geese that laid the golden egg and never cackled". In September 1941, he visited Bletchley Park personally, addressing codebreakers assembled outside the mansion: "In just a few words, with deep emotion, he said how grateful he was to us for all the good work we were doing in the war effort," one of the codebreakers recalled.

The extensive use of electro-magnetic machines designed by Alan Turing and known as the Bombes was increasing the capability of Bletchley Park, but this was not matched by the ability of Alastair Denniston, the head of Bletchley, to obtain the equipment and manpower they needed to exploit the progress they were making. On 21 October 1941, four of the leading codebreakers working on Enigma, Gordon Welchman, Stuart Milner-Barry, Alan Turing and Hugh Alexander, wrote to Churchill personally. "Dear Prime Minister," the letter began, "Some weeks ago you paid us the honour of a visit, and we believe that you regard our work as important … We think, however, that you ought to know that this work is being held up, and in some cases is not being done at all, principally because we cannot get sufficient staff to deal with it. Our reason for writing to you direct is that for months we have done everything that we possibly can through the normal channels, and that we despair of any early improvement without your intervention." Milner-Barry delivered the letter to Downing Street himself and experienced some difficulty persuading Churchill's aides, who could not be briefed on its contents, that it should be passed to the Prime Minister. Eventually he succeeded and Churchill immediately sent his staff one of his infamous "Action This Day" memos, ordering them to "make sure they have all they want extreme priority and report to me that this has been done".

ABOVE Churchill is still wrongly accused of deliberately allowing the bombing of Coventry to go ahead in November 1940 to prevent the Germans discovering that Bletchley Park had broken the German Enigma ciphers.

OPPOSITE Stewart Menzies (on the left), the head of MI6 (seen here with his first wife Avice), briefed Churchill every day on MI6 and Bletchley intelligence.

CHURCHILL AND THE HOLOCAUST

Churchill has been accused of having covered up early evidence of the Holocaust to ensure the Germans did not know that Enigma had been broken. In fact, the reverse is true. Within weeks of the German invasion of the Soviet Union in June 1941, Bletchley Park was breaking messages showing that tens of thousands of Jews were being murdered. Churchill requested a special series of reports on the killings and, despite the danger that it would lead to improved German cipher security, he made one of his most famous speeches to draw attention to the murders, denouncing them as "a crime without a name".

MOST SECRET

GERMAN POLICE.

The Commanding Officer of Police for
South Russia in sending in his report for
23rd August, 1941, says:

The 1 S.S. Brigade took 30 prisoners
in a minor action S.W. of Topiluja. At Luginy
after the burning of the Barracks 5 Communist
Saboteurs were identified.   Police Regiment South
Battalion 314 shot (367) Jews.   In cleaning up
operations South of the Northern Line of Advance
(Rollbahn Nord) 3rd Partisan Battalion may be said
to have been entirely wiped out, 9th Partisan
Battalion half wiped out.

de/G/27.8.41.

Distribution:
    The Director   1 copy
    File   1 copy.

MOST SECRET

GERMAN POLICE.

A report from the BERDITSCHEW KOROSTEN
area mentions that the Russians are
still retiring and burning the villages.

Prisoners taken number 47, Jews shot (1246)
losses nil.

Date 26/8/41.   Report to HIMMLER.

de G/1.9.41.

Distribution :-

    The Director   1 copy.
    File   1 copy.

THIS PAGE Reports on
the killings of Jews on the
Eastern Front produced
specifically for Churchill who
has circled the numbers
killed in red ink.

RIGHT Letter from Desmond Morton, Churchill's intelligence adviser, to Stewart Menzies, "C" or the "Chief" of MI6, requesting that key Enigma reports be sent to him daily.

HW1/1

10, Downing Street,
Whitehall.

MOST SECRET.   September 27, 1940.

Dear C.

    In confirmation of my telephone message, I have been personally directed by the Prime Minister to inform you that he wishes you to send him daily all the ENIGMA messages.

    These are to be sent in a locked box with a clear notice stuck to it "THIS BOX IS ONLY TO BE OPENED BY THE PRIME MINISTER IN PERSON".

    After seeing the messages he will return them to you.

            Yours ever,

           Desmond Morton

P.S. As there will be no check possible here,
      would you please institute a check on receipt
C.   of returned documents to see that you have
      got them all back.

INTELLIGENCE IN THE MIDDLE EAST AND BALKANS

MI6 started the war with four stations in the Middle East, at Cairo, Jerusalem, Baghdad and Aden, expanding these to include Tehran in early 1940.

Iran was also covered by a long-standing arrangement with the Anglo-Iranian Oil Company by which its officials provided intelligence to MI6. There were further stations in the Balkans in Istanbul, Sofia, Bucharest, Athens and Belgrade, of which only Istanbul would remain in place throughout the war. At the start of the war, the head of station in Jerusalem, John Teague, was in charge of the Middle East stations. But the expansion of the Cairo station under cover of the Inter-Services Liaison Department led to its head, Sir David Petrie, taking control of Middle East operations. When Petrie took over MI5 in 1941, he was replaced by Cuthbert Bowlby.

The first critical contribution of British intelligence to the war in the Near and Middle East came in the early spring of 1941, not from MI6 but from Bletchley Park, which broke the Italian navy Enigma cipher. This enabled the codebreakers to decipher the entire orders of the Italian fleet which was on its way to attack the British naval convoys taking troops between Egypt and Greece. This remarkable coup allowed Admiral Sir Andrew Cunningham, the Commander-in-Chief, Mediterranean Fleet, to intercept the Italians off Cape Matapan on the night of 28 March 1941. Three British battleships destroyed a complete Italian cruiser squadron, and the Italian fleet never ventured out of port again.

At the same time, the codebreakers were picking up indications from messages enciphered using the German railways Enigma of large-scale German troop movements in what was clearly preparation for invasions of Yugoslavia and Greece. In April 1941, German troops swept through Yugoslavia and into Greece. The codebreakers fed the German plans to British commanders, but the British and Greek troops faced insuperable odds and were forced to retreat. Bletchley also picked up details of the German plans for an airborne attack on Crete, including the date it was to be launched, 20 May 1941. These were passed to General Bernard Freyberg, the New Zealand commander in Crete, disguised as a report from an MI6 agent inside the German headquarters in Athens. Freyberg did not have the resources to fight off a sustained attack, but the "MI6 agent's report" robbed the Germans of any element of surprise – Freyberg allegedly looked at his watch when the German paratroopers began dropping from their aircraft and said: "Right on time". His men were able to pick off the enemy paratroopers at will, causing carnage and considerably delaying what was an inevitable Allied defeat.

"Crete was an example of how knowing a great deal, through the Red Enigma cipher, didn't necessarily lead to the correct results," said John Herivel, one of the leading Hut 6 codebreakers. "What did happen was that they had such enormous difficulty in taking Crete and suffered such enormous losses that Hitler decided he wouldn't try a parachute descent in that strength again."

MI6 in Cairo began the war with a belief that they could tap into the very strong French networks in Syria, Lebanon, Iraq and Iran. But the invasion of France in May 1940 put initial limitations on MI6 activity in Syria and Lebanon. The United States consuls in the region, who were themselves gathering intelligence, were helpful and the Free French were

OPPOSITE MI6 had an arrangement with the Anglo-Iranian Oil Company whereby its employees in Iran provided intelligence about the area.

also soon able to set up their own networks. This ensured that MI6 had the entire order of battle of the Vichy French forces in Syria ahead of the occupation of the country by British and Free French forces in June 1941, although Teague told London that relations with the Free French were difficult. It was, he said, "like trying to live amicably with a jealous, touchy and domineering wife". Relations were sufficiently strained for MI6 to run an agent into the headquarters of the Free French commander, General Georges Catroux. The agent, who was appropriately codenamed Volcano, was a highly prized asset who provided important information from Catroux's communications with the Free French leader, Charles de Gaulle, on the latter's attitude to the British, which was then passed

back to Churchill in London. MI6 worked very closely with both the Free French and the Polish intelligence service throughout the Middle East and, despite the occasional tensions, this ensured good coverage. The tensions were not just with the French and the Polish: Nigel Clive, who spent two years at the MI6 station in Baghdad, later described the "bickering and jealousy" between MI6, SOE and MI5 as each tried to secure more influence than the others over events in Iraq. Nevertheless, the Baghdad station seems to have been productive, warning throughout the first three months of 1941 that a coup to install an Iraqi leader sympathetic to Germany was imminent. The warnings were ignored, but fortunately the uprising was quashed by British troops.

The MI6 Cairo station sent a number of officers behind enemy lines in Yugoslavia and Greece to collect intelligence and to link up with resistance movements, a difficult task since the partisans in both countries were split between right-wing royalists and communists. In the summer of 1943, Clive went to Cairo and secured a place for himself on the MI6 team that was to be sent to Yugoslavia, but ultimately was instead sent to Greece to collect intelligence on the German order of battle there. He parachuted into Greece weighed down by a money

ESPIONAGE WARS IN TURKEY

During the Second World War, neutral Turkey seethed with spies. MI6 ranged up against the German Abwehr, which scored a notable success in recruiting Elyesa Bazna, the valet of the British ambassador, Sir Hughe Knatchbull-Hugessen. Codenamed Cicero, Bazna provided the Germans with photographs of up to 150 top-secret documents between September 1943 and March 1944, when the leak was discovered and an investigation put in place. Considering that Knatchbull-Hugessen had described MI6 as "a cancer it was desirable to remove from the diplomatic body", the MI6 officers based in Turkey might have been forgiven for any feelings of *schadenfreude*. This was particularly so given that, while Knatchbull-Hugessen presented the Germans with an espionage coup, they were busy turning the tables through an Abwehr "walk-in" run by Nicholas Elliott, an MI6 officer based in Ankara. Dr Erich Vermehren, who was anti-Nazi and wanted to defect with his wife, first made contact in January 1944 and over a four-day period photographed documents detailing all the current Abwehr operations in Turkey and throughout the Middle East. Elliott smuggled Vermehren, his wife and two other anti-Nazi Abwehr officers out to Cairo via Noel Rees's escape lines from the fishing village of Khioste near Izmir in western Turkey.

ABOVE Bletchley Park broke the Italian navy messages which allowed the Royal Navy to win the Battle of Matapan.

belt containing a hundred gold sovereigns, a traditional British method of winning support from warring factions. The first difficulty he faced was in persuading SOE officers already on the ground and the resistance fighters he was working with that he could be trusted; his predecessor had been shot in the belief that he was a traitor, an allegation that remained unproven. But Clive was successful in his mission, setting up a network of agents stretching across southwestern Greece and Corfu who gathered information on the activities of the German 22nd Mountain Corps; unusually for MI6, they also conducted ambushes of German convoys and collected further intelligence from prisoners they took during these attacks. One of the most romantic of the MI6 missions in the region was the piratical station at Khioste in southern Turkey run by Noel Rees, who used local fishing boats known as caiques to run MI6 agents to Greece and to provide escape lines for thousands of British and Greek soldiers who had escaped from the Germans.

ABOVE The British codebreakers were able to predict the German airborne invasion of Crete to the precise minute.

LEFT Captain Cuthbert Bowlby RN ran the Cairo headquarters of the Inter-Services Liaison Department, the standard military cover for MI6.

SOE IN THE MIDDLE EAST AND BALKANS

Section D, the special operations section of MI6, had set up a number of largely ineffective operations in the Balkans run from Istanbul, the main ones being in Romania, where attempts were made to block the Danube at the "Iron Gates", the natural rock gorge through which the river flowed between Romania and Yugoslavia.

ABOVE Royalist Serb general Draža Mihailović was dropped by the British because he was ineffective.

OPPOSITE Fitzroy Maclean, the leader of the UK mission to Tito.

There was also an attempt to repeat a successful First World War British secret service operation in which the Romanian oilfields were largely put out of action by a team of mining and oil engineers. Section D had another office in Cairo preparing operations in the Middle East and Greece, which SOE took over in the summer of 1940 as its regional headquarters, combining command of all regional operations in one location. From the outset, SOE Cairo was riven by petty disagreements and infighting. Very few special operations took place in the Middle East proper, where Cairo's main focus was on propaganda, although a band of Jewish Zionists operating on behalf of SOE in Iraq and Syria had some success. The bulk of the special operations controlled by SOE Cairo took place in Yugoslavia, Greece and Albania through a series of missions known collectively as Force 133.

Although neutral at the start of the war, Yugoslavia was highly vulnerable to German pressure and on 25 March 1941 found itself forced to join the Axis powers. Two days later, the government was overthrown in a coup d'état, infuriating Hitler and leading to a German invasion on 6 April 1941. Bill Hudson, who had previously been in Yugoslavia for Section D, was sent back in by submarine in September and linked up initially with a group of communist resistance fighters known as the Partisans, led by Josip Broz, who had adopted the *nom de guerre* Tito. They helped Hudson make contact with the Chetnik resistance led by the royalist Serb general Draža Mihailović, but he was unable to do anything of substance. Mihailović refused point-blank to co-ordinate operations with Tito and it was very soon clear that each man wanted rid of the other. Mihailović mistrusted Bill Hudson,

confiscating his wireless, and German reprisals, executing 100 Yugoslavs for every German soldier killed, led the Chetniks to cut back on their operations. Cairo then sent in Colonel Bill Bailey, who, like Hudson, had worked in Yugoslavia before the war, to try to get Mihailović to take on the Germans more aggressively and work with Tito's Partisans.

The failure of both Hudson and Bailey to get the Chetniks to take on the Germans more actively led the British to explore the possibility of working more closely with Tito. The SOE officers working in Cairo split into factions, with one side pushing Tito's claims and the others those of Mihailović. Bill Deakin, a young Oxford don, was sent to Yugoslavia to make contact with Tito, followed shortly afterwards by a mission sent in by Churchill rather than SOE and led by the SAS officer Fitzroy Maclean. The mission included the author Evelyn Waugh, whose right-wing views were unlikely to endear him to Tito. But both Deakin and Maclean got on well with the Partisan leader. It was immediately clear to them that while the Chetniks were reluctant to take on the Germans, and had done a deal with the Italians under which both sides agreed not to attack the other, Tito and his Partisans were the ones causing real damage to the Germans.

The arguments over whether the British should have backed Tito or Mihailović continue to the present day, with Mihailović largely presented as having collaborated with the Germans. In fact, the only certain evidence of collaboration with the Germans related to Tito, albeit briefly in early 1943, in a deal that aimed to destroy Mihailović, while the only evidence of the latter's collaboration was in the pragmatic deal with the Italians. Critics of the decision, made by the British Prime Minister Winston Churchill himself in November 1943, to back Tito and drop Mihailović, point out that one of the main advocates of this policy inside SOE's Cairo headquarters was James Klugman, a KGB agent, who played an active role in the recruitment of John Cairncross to the Cambridge spy ring. But the intercepts of German communications in Yugoslavia deciphered at Bletchley Park made clear that Tito was far more effective and this was undoubtedly the deciding factor for Churchill.

The resistance movement in Greece also suffered from rivalry between the communists and the other resistance fighters. The two main groups were the communist Greek People's Liberation Army ELAS under Aris Velouchiotis and the National Republican Greek League EDES under Colonel Napoleon Zervas. Despite this, Greece was the scene of one of the earliest and most dramatic demonstrations of SOE's capabilities, with the destruction in November 1942 of the railway bridge over the Gorgopotamos gorge (see page 93), a joint operation involving both EDES and ELAS. Thereafter, both sides received support from SOE, although ELAS claimed it did not and spent as much time preparing for the post-war future by using the weapons supplied by the British to attack

the republican EDES. The British also enjoyed success working with the resistance in Crete, where Paddy Leigh Fermor, Xan Fielding and Bill Stanley Moss kidnapped the local German commander General Heinrich Kreipe (see below right).

The other main SOE activity in the region was in Albania, where Billy Maclean and David Smiley, Peter Kemp and an astonishingly large number of British officers liaised with both the communist National Liberation Movement, the republican Balli Kombëtar and resistance fighters supporting King Zog. They organized a number of attacks, at first on Italian and then later against German troops, and blew up bridges, sometimes laying their explosives beneath the bridge while the Germans patrolled them above. A full-scale British mission was sent into Albania in mid-1943, led by Brigadier Edmund "Trotsky" Davies; the British serving there subsequently included the actor and film star Anthony Quayle and Julian Amery, who would become a Conservative government minister in the 1950s–70s. But, as elsewhere in the Balkans, the communists – led in Albania by Enver Hoxha – were more interested in killing their resistance rivals in preparation for the creation of their own post-war state than in fighting the Germans.

Force 133 also operated in Italy from July 1943 onwards, ahead of the invading Allied troops, where it provided the communications link between General Eisenhower, the Allied commander, and Marshal Pietro Badoglio, the Italian Prime Minister and military commander, which led in September 1943 to the Italian surrender.

OPPOSITE Communist Partisan leader Tito was backed by the British and went on to lead Yugoslavia until his death in 1980.

BELOW Anthony Quayle, the film star, who served with SOE in Albania.

KIDNAPPING OF A GERMAN GENERAL

Two SOE officers, Paddy Leigh Fermor and Stanley Moss, seen here in German uniform with three Cretan resistance fighters, were inserted into Crete from Egypt in early 1944 to kidnap the German general Friedrich-Wilhelm Müller, who was mistreating local Greeks. By the time they were ready for the operation, in May 1944, Müller had been replaced by General Heinrich Kreipe, but it went ahead anyway. Leigh Fermor and Moss, assisted by Cretan resistance fighters, ambushed Kreipe's car and smuggled him through numerous German checkpoints. At one point, Kreipe began reciting the Roman poet Horace and Leigh Fermor finished off what was the only Latin poem he knew by heart. They eventually got Kreipe out to Egypt.

OPERATION HARLING: THE DESTRUCTION OF THE GORGOPOTAMOS BRIDGE

The first major SOE sabotage operation in occupied Europe was Operation Harling, the destruction of the railway bridge over the Gorgopotamos gorge in northern Greece in November 1942 using explosive charges. It was mounted by a 12-man SOE team, led by Eddie Myers, and 150 Greek guerrillas, in the first and last major joint operation between the communist Greek People's Liberation Army (ELAS) and the National Republican Greek League (EDES). These two groups would soon be fighting each other as much as the enemy. Harling's importance was in its demonstration that SOE, working with resistance groups on the ground, could have an impact in the war.

WORKING WITH THE
AMERICANS

During the inter-war years, intelligence cooperation between the British and Americans was limited and mostly conducted between MI5 and the Federal Bureau of Investigation (FBI).

ABOVE Bill Bundy, US Army intelligence officer at Bletchley Park, who went on to be foreign policy advisor to Presidents Kennedy and Johnson.

ABOVE RIGHT Allen Welsh Dulles, OSS station chief in Bern during the war and later first civilian director of the Central Intelligence Agency.

OPPOSITE A US master sergeant at work at Bletchley Park, where intelligence links with the Americans were strongest.

Indeed, at the end of the First World War, America itself was high on the post-war intelligence priorities for both the War Office and the Admiralty. The Government Code & Cypher School (GC&CS) monitored American diplomatic and naval communications, while MI6 operated on the ground within the United States against Irish nationalists and communists, particularly Indian left-wing activists. Such operations were sometimes carried out in tandem with the United States authorities, but often not, leading J Edgar Hoover, the head of the FBI, to report that the British were "much better informed on radical activities in this country, at least in New York, than the United States government".

But shortly before the Second World War, Admiral Sir Hugh Sinclair, the head of MI6, recognizing that American co-operation was needed against the German and Japanese threats, ordered the head of station in New York to end all activities against the United States. While America would not enter the war until the attack on Pearl Harbor in December 1941, tentative approaches were made to the FBI in the summer of 1940, with a Canadian businessman, William Stephenson, who had worked for Claude Dansey's Z Organization, sent to Washington to discuss an intelligence exchange on German and Japanese threats.

There was at this time no federal foreign human intelligence service, with each department collecting intelligence as it saw fit. There were army and navy signals intelligence departments; indeed in October 1939, the British had suggested working together on German and Japanese codes and ciphers to Op-20-G, the US Navy's codebreaking organization, and had been brutally rebuffed. But in August 1940, during a visit to London, a United States Army delegation suggested co-operation between GC&CS, by now based at Bletchley Park, and the US Army Signal Intelligence Service (SIS). The Americans remained unaware of British progress on both the German Enigma ciphers, and the navy remained reluctant to co-operate, but an American mission travelled to London and then to Bletchley Park in February 1941, paving the way for what would eventually become widespread co-operation.

The army representatives, Abraham Sinkov and Leo Rosen, brought a large amount of material, including a machine that replicated the action of the main Japanese diplomatic machine cipher, the Purple machine, which the United States Army had broken in September 1940. But with Laurance Safford, the head of Op-20-G, accepting the exchange only on sufferance, his representatives Prescott Currier and Robert Weeks were authorized to hand over only the results of the limited American progress on the main Japanese naval cipher, on which the British were in fact more advanced, and told simply "to get whatever you think we should get and have a look around".

The anxieties from the British perspective were just as great. Sir Stewart Menzies, the head of MI6, told Churchill that, with details of United States intelligence operations often making their way into the American media, he had severe concerns over US security and was extremely worried that the vital secret that the British had broken a number of German Enigma ciphers might leak out and lead to the Germans changing their cipher system completely. "I find myself unable to devise any safe means of wrapping up the information in a manner which would not imperil this source," Menzies said. It was "well nigh impossible that the information could have been secured by an agent, and however much we insist that it came from a highly placed source, I greatly doubt the enemy being for a moment deceived, should there be any indiscretion in the USA."

Nevertheless, the Americans were taken to Bletchley Park, briefed on the British work on Enigma and given a paper diagram of the Enigma machine detailing its wiring and how it worked, together with details of the Bombes, the primitive computers used to break the Enigma keys.

This was as much as, if not more than, the Americans provided. The United States Army's copy of a Purple machine was extremely valuable to the British, giving them access to the communications of the Japanese ambassador to Berlin, who was informing his government in Tokyo of what the Germans were planning. Despite Safford's suspicion of the British, Currier, the United States Navy's main representative, recalled an atmosphere of "complete co-operation" and said that the members of the American delegation were shown everything they wanted to see. Co-operation with the United States Army codebreakers was completely uninhibited from this point on, and while co-operation with the United States Navy was often difficult, particularly on Japanese codes and ciphers, when it came to the German navy's Enigma ciphers there was too much of a joint interest in ending the U-boat attacks against the Atlantic convoys for it not to be complete. By the latter stages of the war, American technology ensured that most of the daily naval Enigma keys were broken across the Atlantic by United States Bombes.

The United States did not set up a central intelligence service until June 1942 when the Office of Strategic Services was created, although preparations had been going on since July 1941, when its first head William J Donovan was appointed co-ordinator of information. The OSS was the American equivalent of both MI6 and SOE, and Stephenson, who had taken over as MI6 head of station in New York in June 1941, set up British Security Co-ordination to liaise with OSS on behalf of both MI6 and SOE.

Co-operation between SOE and the OSS was generally good, with the British more experienced in operational technique, and fully prepared to share it, while the Americans had more money for equipment and aircraft, which they also shared. The main difficulties came in Yugoslavia, where the Americans were far more reluctant to back the communist Tito, and in the Far East, where there was a great deal of rivalry and both sides broke agreements made with the other in order to gain the upper hand, to the extent that the official British historian noted that in Thailand (then Siam) the two services seemed to be more at war with each other than with the enemy.

ABOVE LEFT William "Wild Bill" Donovan, head of the Office of Strategic Services, the US equivalent of MI6 and SOE.

ABOVE RIGHT Telford Taylor, head of the US Army liaison at Bletchley and chief US prosecutor at Nuremberg.

OPPOSITE TOP Mark Felt, FBI officer who played an important part in the Double-Cross system. He is better known for his role as "Deep Throat" in the Watergate scandal.

Relations between OSS and MI6 and MI5 were on the whole good, with the United States basing officers in London and taking an increasing part in the Double Cross System as the war progressed, but it was the relationship between Bletchley Park and its American counterparts, based largely on the British breaking of the Enigma ciphers, that formed the basis for the very strong intelligence-sharing relationship between the two countries which continues today.

BRITISH SECURITY CO-ORDINATION

At the beginning of 1941, American entry into the war was seen as inevitable. As a result both the US and Britain wanted to set up an intelligence sharing agreement. So the MI6 station in New York was turned into a much more formal liaison organization called British Security Co-ordination (BSC). It was headed by William Stephenson, a Canadian businessman, seen on the right receiving the US Order for Merit. He had provided MI6 with intelligence in the run-up to the war and had been appointed US head of station in June 1940. BSC was based in the Rockefeller Center on New York's Fifth Avenue; it had the principal role of liaising on behalf of both MI6 and SOE with US intelligence, known from June 1942 as the Office of Strategic Services, which combined intelligence and special operations. BSC also liaised on behalf of MI5 with the FBI and the Royal Canadian Mounted Police (RCMP). But J Edgar Hoover, the head of the FBI, did not trust Stephenson and eventually MI5 set up direct liaisons with both the FBI and the RCMP. Stephenson was not shy of playing up his role, commissioning a flattering official history and glorying under the alleged codename Intrepid, which was in fact simply the telegraphic address of BSC.

BATTLE OF THE ATLANTIC

As the German war machine marched across Europe, Britain became increasingly dependent on convoys to transport supplies across the Atlantic.

The fall of France in June 1940 provided German submarines – U-boats – with easy access to the Atlantic and bases from which to launch attacks on the vital convoys. As Britain relied on these convoys for half of its food requirements and all of its oil, the convoys were obvious targets for the "wolf-packs" of U-boats, which lined up north to south across the shipping routes. Once contact was made with a convoy, the closest U-boats would shadow it, sending out homing signals to draw in the other members of the pack. When all the U-boats were assembled, they pounced en masse on the Allied shipping. The Germans had the added advantage of having broken the Merchant Navy code used by the convoys and they were also reading a great deal of the Royal Navy's operational messages. So the wolf packs knew the routes to be taken by the convoys and could lie in wait.

It was the job of the Admiralty's Operational Intelligence Centre (OIC) to re-route the convoys around the U-boats and to do this it needed Bletchley Park to tell them where the U-boats were. But the German naval Enigma ciphers were more complex than their army and Luftwaffe counterparts. It was not until April 1940 that a naval Enigma codebreaking unit, known as Hut 8, was set up at Bletchley Park, with Alan Turing in charge, assisted by Peter Twinn. By early May, Turing had broken the keys for several days in April but it was impossible to break the cipher in the sort of "real time" that would help the OIC to protect the convoys. By September 1940, with attacks on Allied shipping mounting rapidly, the need to find a sustained break into the U-boat cipher had become imperative.

The solution was still nine months away but a series of "pinches" or captures of German cipher documents in the first half of 1941, in one case snatched by Royal Marine commandos during a raid on the Lofoten Islands, and the discovery that the U-boat messages were also sent on a lower-level hand cipher which was easy to crack, ensured that by June 1941 Turing and his team were able to break the U-boat cipher. The results were truly dramatic. Between March and June 1941, the wolf packs had sunk 282,000 tons of shipping a month. From July, the figure dropped to 120,000 tons a month and by November, when the U-boats were temporarily withdrawn from the Atlantic, to 62,000 tons. Bletchley Park's success in breaking the cipher during this period is estimated to have saved around one and a half million tons of shipping, the equivalent of 350 ships.

But on 1 February 1942, the U-boats introduced a new cipher with four wheels rather than the three normal on the early Enigma machines. This new cipher was dubbed Shark by the Bletchley Park codebreakers and the next ten months, during which only a very few occasional messages were broken, became known as the Shark Blackout. The vital intelligence the OIC had been using to re-route the Atlantic convoys had disappeared. The problems caused by the Shark Blackout were exacerbated by a rise in the number of U-boats in the Atlantic to 40 and the breaking by German codebreakers of the Royal

Navy's Naval Cypher No 3, which was used for most of the Allied communications about the Atlantic convoys.

A week after Shark came into force, the OIC's submarine-tracking room admitted that it was at a loss to say where the U-boats were. With a great deal of work, Hut 8 did manage to solve the keys for two days in late February 1942 and one day in March. But it took six Bombes 17 days to solve each of those settings. Tension began to rise between the Admiralty and Bletchley Park, with senior naval officers accusing the codebreakers of seeing the whole thing as an academic puzzle and failing to realize that the

sailors manning the convoys "lived and moved and had their being in a world vibrant with the noise of battle".

Between February and August 1942, the U-boats were away from the main Atlantic shipping lanes, attacking the convoys on the eastern seaboard of the United States in an operation codenamed Drumbeat. But in August 1942, the wolf packs resumed their attacks on the convoys with 86 U-boats, four times as many as when Shark was introduced. During August and September, they located 21 of the 63 convoys that sailed, sinking 43 ships. They destroyed 485,413 tons of shipping in September, and in October, when there were more than 100 U-boats at sea, sank 619,417 tons.

The Admiralty began to step up the pressure on Bletchley Park to break Shark, with a tersely written note to Hut 8

OPERATION RUTHLESS

Ian Fleming, the creator of James Bond, devised a "cunning scheme" codenamed Operation Ruthless to help Bletchley Park break the Enigma cipher used by the German U-boats. His plan rivalled some of the exploits of his fictional hero. He pencilled his own name as one of the crew who should each be "tough, a bachelor, able to swim", much like Bond. They would dress in Luftwaffe uniforms, made up with blood and bandages, and fly a captured German bomber alongside real Luftwaffe bombers returning home from a raid on London. On the French side of the Channel, they would send out an SOS and ditch in the sea. When a German boat came to rescue them, they would overpower the crew and sail the boat and its precious Enigma machine and keys to Britain. Ruthless was authorized but eventually called off, leaving the leading naval codebreakers Alan Turing and Peter Twinn furious. "Turing and Twinn came to me like undertakers cheated of a nice corpse yesterday, all in a stew about the cancellation of Ruthless," the head of Bletchley Park's naval section, Frank Birch, told Fleming. "Did the authorities realize that there was very little hope, if any, of their deciphering current, or even approximately current, Enigma at all?"

ABOVE U-Boats were the greatest threat to Britain's survival, picking off the Atlantic convoys at will during the second half of 1942.

LEFT Hugh Alexander, the second head of the naval Enigma team in Hut 8 which struggled for more than ten months to break Shark.

RIGHT The four-rotor German naval Enigma cipher machine, codenamed Shark by the Bletchley Park codebreakers.

complaining that the U-boat campaign was "the only one campaign which Bletchley Park are not at present influencing to any marked extent and it is the only one in which the war can be lost unless BP do help".

But the solution to Shark was already in place. Two days after the Admiralty memorandum, a "pinch" of two German "short signal" codebooks arrived at Bletchley, providing new cribs for the U-boat messages. The books had been recovered from the U-559 which was scuttled by its crew after being attacked by the British destroyer HMS *Petard* off the Egyptian coast. Lieutenant Anthony Fasson and Able-Seaman Colin Grazier swam to the submarine before it sank and managed to recover its signal documents. They were joined by a 16-year-old NAAFI (Navy, Army and Air Force Institutes) boy, Tommy Brown. He stayed by the conning tower and succeeded in getting out with the codebooks. But Fasson and Grazier went down with the submarine. They were both awarded the George Cross posthumously. Brown, a civilian, received the George Medal. The medals were well-deserved; their heroism was vital in helping to end the U-boat blackout.

On Sunday 13 December 1942, the codebreakers got back into Shark. The breaks were intermittent and some days' keys were never deciphered, but from then on Shark was broken on most days. During the first five months of 1943, nearly 100 U-boats were sunk, forcing their withdrawal from the North Atlantic, safeguarding convoys and giving the Allies a year to build up supplies in preparation for D-Day.

ABOVE Tommy Brown, the 16-year-old NAAFI boy who helped to "pinch" the vital codebooks from the U-559.

LEFT *Petard*, a P-class destroyer, sank the U-559 off Egypt to obtain the vital information the codebreakers needed.

WOMEN
IN THE SECRET WAR

Although the First World War had seen a number of young women involved in the intelligence wars, most notably Mata Hari, Edith Cavell, Gertrude Bell and a number of young Belgian and French women who took part in the highly successful train-watching operations, the Second World War saw women taking a much greater role.

The best known are those who worked alongside the Special Operations Executive, many of them as members of the First Aid Nursing Yeomanry (FANY). There were also a number of much less well-known women who worked for MI6 and at Bletchley Park, where not only were several of the leading codebreakers women, but the majority of the back-up staff were female, including around 2,000 members of the Women's Royal Naval Service (WRENs), the bulk of whom operated the bombes, without which the Enigma cipher would not have been broken so successfully.

A single short chapter could not do justice to the many, but of those involved in special operations and resistance several names stand out. Pearl Witherington, who had been brought up in France, worked with Maurice Southgate in the Loire valley; when he was captured shortly before D-Day, she took charge of several thousand resistance fighters, who harassed German troops trying to move from southern France towards the fighting in the north. She was so effective that the Germans put a one-million-franc price tag on her head.

She was originally recommended for a Military Cross but was deemed ineligible because she was a woman. Offered a civilian MBE, she declined, saying, "There was nothing civil about what I did."

Violette Szabo, whose husband had died at El Alamein, volunteered to be parachuted into France in April 1944 to work with the French resistance in southwest France. She was twice arrested by the Germans, each time managing to get away. But on 10 June 1944, she was captured by the Gestapo, albeit not without a fight. She was interrogated and tortured but refused to give anything away and was eventually taken to the Ravensbrück concentration camp where she was executed and incinerated. She was just 23 years old.

Szabo was not the only female SOE agent to die in a German concentration camp. Noor Inayat Khan, codenamed Madeleine, was sent to France on 16 June 1943 to be a wireless operator for the Cinema sub-circuit of the Prosper line, but the network was compromised and four months later she was captured. She was taken to Dachau where she was subsequently executed. On 6

RIGHT Margaret Reid, who joined MI6 in the late 1930s and was sent to Berlin. She operated in Norway and Lisbon during the war.

OPPOSITE The majority of those who worked at Bletchley Park were women. Here they are testing out possible solutions using an actual Enigma machine.

July 1944, Andrée Borrel, Vera Leigh, Sonya Olschanezky and Diana Rowden, all SOE agents captured while working with the French resistance, were taken to Natzweiler concentration camp, where they were injected with phenol and incinerated. Mention should also be made of Odette Sansom, who was arrested by the Gestapo while working in France with her lover and future husband Peter Churchill. Despite claiming to be Mrs Churchill and related to the British Prime Minister, she was interrogated, tortured and eventually sent to Ravensbrück, although she survived.

Bravery was never in short supply among such women. Countess Krystyna Gizycka, alias Christine Granville, was originally recruited as an agent for MI6, travelling into occupied Poland to collect intelligence. She was sent into France in July 1944 for SOE to act as courier for Francis Cammaerts, who was in charge of resistance operations east of the River Rhône. When Cammaerts, his deputy Xan Fielding and a French colleague were arrested by the Gestapo, Gizycka rang up a Belgian Gestapo interpreter, offering him a two-million-franc bribe and warning him what would happen to him if he did not get them released. She then drove all three men from the prison, an act of bravery for which she was subsequently awarded both the George Medal and the *Croix de Guerre*.

Large numbers of women worked at Bletchley Park, although only a few were among the leading codebreakers who actually broke into systems, rather than those who broke the day's keys. These were Mavis Batey and Margaret Rock, who both worked with Dilly Knox, the chief cryptographer, in the Research Section and then on Abwehr Enigmas. Batey was responsible for the break into the Italian Enigma cipher which provided the British with the Italian navy's plans for the Battle of Matapan, leading to the destruction of the Italian fleet in what Churchill described as the greatest British naval victory since Trafalgar. Joan Murray worked in the naval Enigma section Hut 8 with Alan Turing, to whom she was briefly engaged, and was involved in the battles to break the U-boat Enigma ciphers.

THE MISS MARPLE OF THE SECRET WAR

Few of the very remarkable women who worked for MI6 during the war were quite as indomitable as Margaret Hasluck (right). One of a number of such women who worked for MI6 during the First World War – others included Edith Cavell and Gertrude Bell – she was an archaeologist and anthropologist. Her husband, FW Hasluck, himself a famous archaeologist and Middle East expert, worked with Compton Mackenzie in Athens but died tragically young. Margaret then worked for Mansfield Cumming, the first head of the service in London, and after the war moved to Albania, where she became an expert on that country and its people. All the evidence suggests she was working for British intelligence in the months before the Italian occupation of Albania. When the Italians expelled her as a spy, she went to neutral Turkey and from there ran a network of agents inside Albania on behalf of MI6. In 1942, when SOE wanted to send David Smiley and Billy Maclean into Albania, the 57-year-old Hasluck was appointed to head the Albanian section in SOE's Cairo headquarters. She not only tutored Smiley and Maclean in Albanian but also gave them personal letters to her contacts asking them to assist the two SOE officers.

ABOVE Mavis Batey was one of the leading codebreakers.

ABOVE Christine Granville (Gizycka), who worked for SOE in France, rescued her boss Francis Cammaerts and two colleagues from the Gestapo.

There were fewer women working as senior intelligence officers within MI5 and MI6. The most prominent was Jane Archer, a leading MI5 officer who was one of the leading experts within British intelligence on its Soviet counterparts. She had interviewed General Walter Krivitsky, a major defector from the Soviet intelligence service, the NKVD. When she was sacked by MI5 for being too honest about the failings of a senior officer, she was immediately taken on by MI6 and put to work alongside Kim Philby, then a senior officer in the MI6 counter-espionage branch, Section V, but already himself a Soviet agent and leading member of the Cambridge spy ring. Krivitsky told Archer that one of the Soviet agents was a young man who had worked as a journalist during the Spanish Civil War. This fitted Philby's description and he

later recalled that being told Archer was to work with him gave him "a nasty shock", but she never connected him with the young journalist mentioned by Krivitsky.

There were many MI6 female agents and officers, of whose names only a few have been released. Many were secretaries until the war broke out, at which point they took on much more onerous work. These included Margaret Reid, who played a vital role in maintaining contact with London and passing and receiving intelligence on the Nazi invasion of Norway in April 1940 while her boss Frank Foley, head of station in Oslo, retreated with the Norwegian High Command. The link between Foley and MI6, maintained using the service's book code, was the first time the intelligence reports from Bletchley Park were sent to a unit fighting in the field.

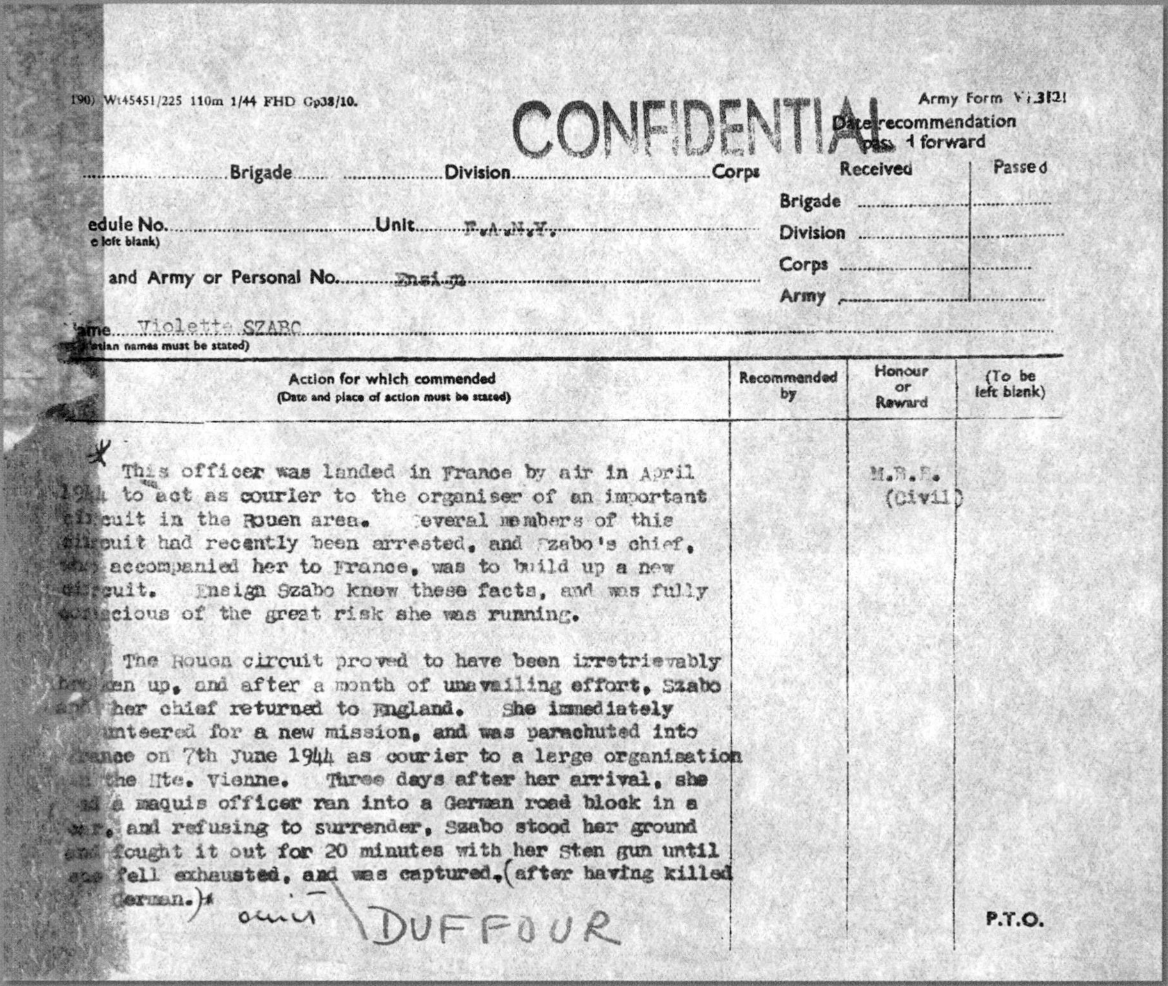

CONFIDENTIAL

Army Form Wi 3121

190) Wt45451/225 110m 1/44 FHD Gp38/10.

.... Brigade .... Division............. .... Corps

edule No....................... Unit......... F.A.N.Y.
c left blank)

and Army or Personal No............ Ensign

Name... Violette SZABO
(istian names must be stated)

	Date recommendation passed forward	
	Received	Passed
Brigade	....	....
Division	....	....
Corps	....	....
Army	....	....

Action for which commended (Date and place of action must be stated)	Recommended by	Honour or Reward	(To be left blank)
This officer was landed in France by air in April 1944 to act as courier to the organiser of an important circuit in the Rouen area. Several members of this circuit had recently been arrested, and Szabo's chief, who accompanied her to France, was to build up a new circuit. Ensign Szabo knew these facts, and was fully conscious of the great risk she was running.		M.B.E. (Civil)	
The Rouen circuit proved to have been irretrievably broken up, and after a month of unavailing effort, Szabo and her chief returned to England. She immediately volunteered for a new mission, and was parachuted into France on 7th June 1944 as courier to a large organisation in the Hte. Vienne. Three days after her arrival, she and a maquis officer ran into a German road block in a car, and refusing to surrender, Szabo stood her ground and fought it out for 20 minutes with her Sten gun until she fell exhausted, and was captured (after having killed German.)			
omis \DUFFOUR			P.T.O.

ABOVE The commendation for SOE agent Violette Szabo for an MBE for her work in France. She was executed in Ravensbrück concentration camp in February 1945.

MI9 ESCAPE AND EVASION

MI9, the organization which taught Allied aircrew how to evade capture and assisted British prisoners of war to escape from German prison camps, was set up in December 1939 under Major Norman Crockatt. Initially, it had the twin role of helping British and Allied prisoners or evaders escape from behind enemy lines and of controlling the interrogation of enemy prisoners of war.

In December 1941, the interrogation of enemy prisoners was split off to become the responsibility of MI9 and from then on MI9 dealt solely with running escape lines for Allied escapers and evaders and collecting intelligence from them, not just when they returned to the UK, but even while they remained in the camps.

Run by a small section that was in effect part of MI6 and came under the abrasive assistant chief of MI6 Claude Dansey, MI9 lectured aircrew who were to bomb behind enemy lines on what to do if they were shot down and provided them with maps printed on silk scarves and German identity papers and money. Selected aircrew and troops picked out during the pre-operational lectures were taught simple codes by which to pass intelligence back to the United Kingdom. MI9's coding sub-section invented fictional characters and would write to those trained in codes who were captured, affecting to be a long-lost aunt or an old school-friend concerned over their welfare. As much information as was available was then sent back encoded in the return letter. MI9 also sent money, maps, civilian clothes, compasses and hacksaws into the prisoner-of-war camps.

Perhaps the most inventive assistance provided to MI9 came from Jasper Maskelyne, a member of a famous family of stage magicians, who lectured some 200,000 Allied airmen on techniques to use in escape and evasion. He is also credited with inventing a number of different items which hid compasses, cutting tools and other escape items, although he was not alone in creating these. A veteran of the First World War, Clayton Hutton was the initial architect of the escape items, which began with maps produced by the map publisher Bartholomew and printed on white silk scarves. The vast bulk of RAF aircrew

LEFT Claude Dansey, Deputy chief of MI6, took overall charge of MI9 to ensure that the latter's escape lines did not compromise MI6 agents.

OPPOSITE The magician Jasper Maskelyne designed MI9 escape kits hidden in parcels of food and games sent to British prisoners of war in Germany.

took one of Hutton's silk scarves with them on missions. More than two million tiny brass compasses were hidden in fountain pens or buttons. Hutton arranged for all razor blades sold by the NAAFI to be magnetized and to have a tiny dent punched

in their centre so that they could be placed on the tip of a pen or pencil and rotate to point north. Perhaps his most influential device was "the escape box", which included malted milk tablets, boiled sweets, bars of chocolate, matches, Benzedrine tablets to provide energy, water-purifying tablets, a rubber water bottle, a razor with a magnetized blade, a needle and thread and a fishing line (although very few fish are believed to have been caught).

Since the operation of escape lines involved running agents abroad, from December 1941 onwards MI9's activities were controlled heavily by MI6. As a result, MI9 led a dual existence, as the ninth department of the Directorate of Military Intelligence and as P15 of MI6, the fifteenth of the MI6 production sections, with Dansey having a veto over everything it did. It was run by James Langley, the head of P15, whose father had served with MI6 during the First World War. Langley's deputy was Airey Neave, who had himself escaped from one of the most prominent

of the German prisoner-of-war camps, Colditz Castle. Neave was later a leading Conservative politician and was assassinated in 1979 in a bomb attack by Irish terrorists.

The relationship between Dansey and MI9 was a difficult one, based on the MI6 experience during the First World War, when Edith Cavell, an MI6 agent in Brussels, was caught and shot as a direct result of the assistance she gave to Allied servicemen attempting to escape from Belgium. Langley later wrote that this "seemed to dictate the whole attitude" of MI6 towards P15/MI9. "The section had great difficulty in obtaining suitable agents for the work," Langley said. "Most of our contacts with the French, Belgian and Dutch intelligence services were originally arranged by MI6, whose ignorance of and lack of interest in the rapidly increasing evader problem spread to their opposite numbers in the Allied services. This apathy towards the work of P15, however, was probably the main cause of its considerable success, for, to achieve anything, it had to work on its own. It led to the section running an organization which few people in England knew anything about, but which had a marked influence on public opinion on the Continent. The better class of underground worker distrusted his own intelligence services and preferred to enrol in an escape movement which had no political bias and a more human aspect than mere espionage. The section, therefore, was able eventually to obtain a remarkably high standard of agents without the assistance of either MI6 or of the allied intelligence services."

The first of the main European escape lines was the so-called Pat or PAO line, run by the Belgian Albert-Marie Edmond Guérisse, by training a doctor, by inclination a maverick adventurer, who took the name Patrick Albert O'Leary. It was in fact several separate lines, one of which ran from Paris through Limoges to Toulouse and then down over the Pyrenees into Spain. Another ran from Paris to Clermont-Ferrand and then on to Beziers and Perpignan, either crossing the Pyrenees into Spain or going by boat to Gibraltar. The third ran from Paris to Dijon and through Lyons to Marseilles and then along the coast to Perpignan.

BRILLIANTLY AUDACIOUS ESCAPE

David Pelham James was a lieutenant in the Royal Naval Volunteer Reserve (RNVR) commanding a motor gunboat operating out of Felixstowe in February 1943 when his boat was sunk off the Hook of Holland and he was rescued and taken prisoner by a German trawler. He was taken to Marlag, the naval prisoner-of-war camp at Westertimke, northeast of Bremen. Taking advantage of the proliferation of uniforms worn by officers in the armed forces of Germany's Eastern European allies, James escaped from the camp wearing his RNVR uniform with papers identifying him as Lieutenant Ivan Bagerov of the Royal Bulgarian Navy. The name Bagerov was chosen because it sounded Bulgarian and was easy to remember, being a deliberate adaptation of "Bugger Off". James slipped out of the camp during bathing parade. His fellow inmates used a dummy to take his place while he climbed out of a window and made his way north, intent on taking a boat to Sweden. Unfortunately he was spotted by a sentry at the docks and returned to Marlag. Undaunted by his experience, he served his term in solitary confinement and a few weeks later repeated the trick, this time making his way successfully to Stockholm. James was later Conservative MP for North Dorset.

LEFT Major Airey Neave escaped from Colditz and then worked for MI9 in London. Later a Conservative MP, he was murdered by Irish terrorists.

OPPOSITE TOP Badminton rackets containing German money, maps and other escape equipment were sent to British PoWs in Colditz.

OPPOSITE BOTTOM The De Havilland Mosquito factory was disguised by Jasper Maskelyne and his team so that it would appear from above (and therefore to German planes) that Agent ZigZag had succeeded in his mission to blow it up (see page 114-115).

THE DOUBLE CROSS SYSTEM

THE DOUBLE CROSS SYSTEM

BELOW JC Masterman, the Oxford academic and senior MI5 officer who chaired the Double Cross Committee.

The Double Cross system originated with a suggestion at the start of the war by Dick White, a future head of both MI5 and MI6, that captured German agents should be "turned" to work as double agents for British intelligence.

At this stage the idea was merely to find out from observing and analysing the questions asked by the Germans what they did and did not know.

One of the earliest opportunities to turn a German agent came with the arrest of Arthur Owens, a Welsh businessman who travelled frequently to Germany and had volunteered in 1936 to collect intelligence for MI6. His intelligence was of no use and he was therefore dropped, but he later got back in touch with MI6 to inform them that he had managed to get himself recruited as a German agent, claiming to have done so in order to penetrate the German intelligence service on behalf of the British. However, interception of his correspondence with his German controller suggested he was playing the two services off against each other.

On the outbreak of war, Owens was arrested and agreed to work as a double agent under the cover-name of Snow. His controller was Lieutenant-Colonel Tommy "Tar" Robertson of MI5, who was to become the effective head of the Double Cross system. Snow had been given a radio transmitter by the Germans in January 1939, which he handed over to MI5 immediately. He had also been given a very primitive cipher, and interception of messages that used similar ciphers uncovered more Abwehr agents. As a result, by the end of 1940 Robertson had a dozen double agents under his control, with MI6 running others overseas, and the main aim had become to use them to feed false information to the Germans that would deceive them as to Allied intentions.

A "Most Secret" committee, including representatives of MI5, MI6 and naval, military and air intelligence, was set up to decide what information should be fed back to the Germans and to coordinate it all so that the Germans received an entirely false picture of Allied plans and operations. It was called the XX Committee, although it swiftly became known as the Twenty Committee, or the Twenty Club, from the Roman numeral suggested by the double-cross sign. It met once a week in the MI5 headquarters, initially in Wormwood Scrubs prison, but subsequently at 58 St James's Street, London, and was chaired by JC Masterman, a leading historian and future vice-chancellor of Oxford University.

Initially, with the threat of a German invasion dominating the atmosphere in London, it was decided that the "intelligence" provided by the double agents should be used to give an impression of quite how strong Britain's defences were. But by the beginning of 1941, it was clear that more could be done with the double agents. They could be used to deceive the Germans,

ABOVE Lieutenant-Colonel Tommy "Tar" Robertson, head of B1a, was the MI5 officer in day-to-day charge of the Double Cross system.

to provide them with misleading information that would give Allied forces an advantage in the field.

The MI5 and MI6 officers handling the double agents needed to know what information they could give to their agents to build up their reputations with the Germans. Much of it was "chicken feed", unimportant information that would give the Abwehr a sense that its agents were doing something and had access to intelligence, without telling them anything really harmful to the war effort. But mixed among this were key pieces of specious or misleading information, designed to build up a false picture of what the British were doing.

The committee's task was to co-ordinate this work. They supervised the system but they did not run the individual agents. That was done by the MI5 and MI6 officers. "I was in touch with the Germans probably two or three times a day by radio and so I had to move fairly quickly," said Hugh Astor, one of the MI5 agent-runners. "So the approving authorities were not the actual Twenty Committee because it only sat once a week.

AGENT ZIGZAG

Eddie Chapman was a crook and a womanizer who earned enough money from safecracking before the war to enable him to live the life of a wealthy playboy, mixing with people like Noel Coward and Marlene Dietrich. In early 1939, he was forced to go on the run to Jersey, but was arrested and jailed after breaking into a local nightclub. When the Germans invaded the island, Chapman offered to spy for them. He was trained as an Abwehr agent and sent to the United Kingdom on a mission to blow up the De Havilland factory at Hatfield in Hertfordshire, which built the Mosquito bomber. Chapman immediately gave himself up. He was taken over by MI5, given the covername ZigZag and told to make contact with the Germans and tell them he was preparing to carry out his mission. A deception operation was mounted to make it look to German aerial reconnaissance aircraft as If the factory had been blown up and a newspaper article was planted reporting the explosion. Chapman was then sent to meet his German controllers, travelling via the neutral capital of Lisbon, and was taken to an Abwehr safe house in Norway where he was told that

he had won the Iron Cross for his work in Britain. On his return to the UK he was used to report false data on the effect of the German V1 and V2 rocket attacks to make them miss their targets, but Chapman was found to have discussed his role as a double agent with a friend in the criminal fraternity and was immediately dropped.

I would get approval from people who were on the committee and every week I and others who were actually active would prepare a short report for the committee saying what we were doing and what we had done."

While the response of the Abwehr controllers to the double agents' reports helped the Twenty Committee to work out where the gaps in the Germans' knowledge lay, it did not tell them whether or not the deliberately misleading information the agents were sending was believed. But in December 1941, Dilly Knox, one of the least known of those who worked at Bletchley Park but a brilliant codebreaker in both the First and Second World Wars, managed to break the complex four-rotor Abwehr Enigma. Knox was dying of cancer at the time he achieved the breakthrough, but it was probably one of the most important made at Bletchley. It allowed Bletchley Park to intercept the messages being passed along the lines by the German agent handlers back to their headquarters in Hamburg, proving to the officers running the Double Cross system that the Germans believed everything they were told by their agents in the United Kingdom.

Nevertheless, the breaking of the Enigma cipher brought a new problem for the committee. The release of any material from Bletchley Park was controlled extremely strictly by MI6 in order to safeguard the Ultra secret. The fact that the "unbreakable" Enigma ciphers had been broken had to be protected at all costs. The MI6 representative on the committee

BELOW Dusko Popov, codename Tricycle, an MI6 agent in Yugoslavia, got the Germans to send him to the UK as a spy and then worked against them.

ABOVE Dilwyn (Dilly) Knox, the brilliant Bletchley Park codebreaker who broke the Abwehr Enigma cypher.

was Felix Cowgill, the head of Section V, the MI6 counter-espionage division. He refused to allow some members of the Twenty Committee to see the material, making it impossible for them to do their job. This led to a major row between MI5 and MI6 which was only solved when Cowgill was replaced by Frank Foley, who ensured all members of the committee saw any Bletchley Park material they needed.

By the beginning of 1943, the information collected from the Abwehr messages deciphered at Bletchley Park showed that the Germans were completely fooled by everything that the double agents were telling them. It also allowed Robertson to state categorically that MI5 now controlled all the German agents operating in Britain, paving the way for a series of spectacular deception operations culminating in the "bodyguard of lies" that ensured the D-Day invasion of Europe was successful.

MEMORANDUM ON THE "DOUBLE AGENT" SYSTEM

1.   A fairly extensive "double agent " system has been built up by M.I.5 and M.I.6, but there is considerable difficulty in keeping it in existence, mainly because the Service Departments (for obvious reasons) are chary of releasing sufficient information to the enemy for him to retain confidence in the agents. We submit, however, that it is possible to secure that the losses involved in releasing information are outweighed by the gains accruing from the successful working of the system.

2. ADVANTAGES TO BE GAINED FROM THE "DOUBLE AGENT" SYSTEM

(1) For Counter-Espionage

During 1914-1918 the Censorship and the British Intelligence Service abroad provided the bulk of the information for counter-espionage work. Postal communication has now ceased to play quite so important a part in espionage work, whilst, since the German conquest of the Continent, the British Secret Service operates under grave difficulties. In these circumstances the "double agent" system has acquired a new and greater importance in counter-espionage work. It enables us to gain an insight into the personnel, methods, and means of communication of the German espionage organization in this country, while we are also led to the discovery of other agents supplied to the "double agent" as contacts. These at a chosen moment can be eliminated or brought under our control.

By building up a "double agent " organization and establishing the enemy's confidence in it, we limit other enemy espionage activities. Incidentally, as the enemy is forced to run the system on a cash basis, funds are diverted which might otherwise be expended on enterprises not under our control.

(2) For Cypher Work

When "double agents" carry out wireless transmission in cypher the enemy is encouraged to believe in the security of his Secret Service cyphers. It is particularly important at the present time, when we are far advanced in the understanding of certain German cyphers, to retain these cyphers in use. Messages from a whole network of German Secret Service wireless stations (used both for espionage and operations) have become comprehensible in the course of the last few months and M.I.5 and M.I.6 have in consequence been enabled to build up a picture of the enemy organization on the Continent and to gain advance information of intended enterprises against this country.

It is also possible that new German cyphers may be broken if we are able through our "double agents" to "plant" information which comes back to us in cypher through the German Secret Serbice wireless.

(3) For Operations

From the questionnaires, some of which are supplied in great detail to "double agents", Service experts can frequently comprehend how much information is already at the disposal of the enemy, and can sometimes make accurate guesses at his intended obje

More important still is the fact that if, and only if, confidence on the enemy's side has been established in a particular "double agent", it will be pos   ropriate moment to mislead the enemy by false   large sca

RIGHT AND FOLLOWING PAGES

An MI5 memorandum on the double agent system, written in December 1940 and appealing for assistance from the three services in providing genuine but harmless information that could be used to enhance the double agents' reputation with their Abwehr agent handlers.

-2-

military operations. When such a moment arrives there should be
no hesitation in sacrificing a "double agent" or group of "double
agents" if important operational results are to be expected from
the sacrifice.

3. The present problem

M.I.5 and M.I.6 must emphasize that only by constant planning in advance and by the maintenance of an adequate flow of con-
sistent and plausible reports to the enemy can the "double agent"
system be kept in being and made available for effective use.
This policy, no doubt, involves the taking of certain risks, but
we submit that the advantages, actual and prospective, which may
be gained are sufficient justification for taking these risks.

We have at the moment two main groups of "double agents"
working from this country. The first and more important is in
wireless communication with the German Secret Service abroad.
The second communicates by personal contact and by secret writing
by air mail, mainly to the German organization in Lisbon. There
are also other agents working abroad.
From our experience of these two systems we can say that
most of the information required by the German Secret Service
relates to air matters. Latterly, and doubtless in view of German
air attacks and the projected invasion of this country, the German
Secret Service has been asking specific questions about the location of factories, military movements, air-raid damage and the like.
Such questions raise the issue of risk to life and property versus
Intelligence value in its most direct from. Are we really secur-
ing sufficient advantages to compensate for the information which
we give to the enemy? The present problem is, in fact, to find
a suitable plan which will ensure that we gain more (or with good
fortune much more) on the swings than we lose on the roundabouts.

4. Possible future lines of development

1. The "double agents" could be graded and developed in
accordance with the importance attached to them. Subsidiary and
less important agents could then be used on a short term basis
with the expectation of their early eclipse and for the deliberate
and immediate misleading of the enemy in matters of detail. The
very few really important agents - especially those who have been
in the confidence of the German Secret Service for some time -
should be the ones entrusted with the handing over of such accurate
information as can, after due consideration by the Service
Departments, be released. These agents should be held in
readiness and at the disposal of the Service Departments for a
large scale deception which could at a critical moment be of
paramount operational importance.

2. In order to build up the important agents into positions
whence at a given moment they can mislead the enemy with the
greatest effect, it is necessary to have some idea of the form
which this deception will have to take. If, for example, the
handing over of false battle positions or large-scal troop
movements is contemplated, our most important "double agents" must
gradually be provided with suitable military contacts from whom
they could derive important military information; if a political
deception is contemplated they would have to be provided with
political contacts. In any case a condition of success would be
that all such contacts were made gradually and over a fairly
long period.

3. Information relating to factory sites, military defence
positions and be   f all kinds should mainly be
entrusted   e agents". Through them it
should be   ices to mislead the enemy.

-3-

For example apparently accurate information could be given
which would in fact refer to dummy targets in the vicinity of a
site, whose exact position had been asked for by the German
Secret Service. For this purpose the co-operation of Colonel
Turner's department would be essential. Alternatively really
accurate information about a site might be provided, and a hot
reception prepared for the expected German raiders. In any
case it is suggested that dummy sites which are prepared to
attract German raiders should be pin-pricked on the maps which
the German Secret Service has provided to certain "double agents".

5.   Up to the present the chief function of M.I.5 and M.I.6
in this matter has been to provide the machinery with which to
mislead the enemy and to invite the Service Departments to plan
for its use. But there is a real danger that the "double agent"
system which has been built up may be allowed to collapse
because no adequate use is made of it. The present committee
is convened to prevent this waste of effort. Its main objects
are to co-ordinate suggestions from its members for making full
use of the machinery provided; to construct plans developed
from these suggestions; and, if necessary, to press for the
putting of these plans into operation.

M.I.5 (B.2a)

27th December, 1940.

BELOW False identity card
for Eddie Chapman, the
British double-cross agent
codenamed ZigZag.

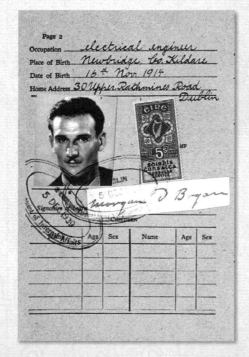

119

INTELLIGENCE
IN THE FAR EAST

OPPOSITE The Purple machine which was used to decipher the main high-grade Japanese diplomatic cipher.

BELOW Brigadier Philip Bowden-Smith, the head of MI6 in India in 1944–45.

British intelligence on the Far East did not have a good start to the war. The stringent cutbacks during the 1920s and early 1930s had forced MI6 to concentrate largely on the activities of Moscow-controlled networks that were spreading communism across China and Southeast Asia using intelligence collected by the Government Code & Cypher School (GC&CS), then based alongside MI6 at its London headquarters in Broadway Buildings.

GC&CS was able to intercept and decipher Japanese diplomatic, naval and military messages throughout the 1930s, but MI6 had very little representation in the Far East.

If human intelligence on Japanese operations was scanty, the codebreakers were able to keep on top of the Japanese military, naval and diplomatic ciphers through an outstation based first in Hong Kong and then, from August 1939, in Singapore. British codebreakers led by John Tiltman, the head of the military codebreaking and intelligence section at Bletchley Park, were entirely on top of all the main Japanese military ciphers, including the invaluable military attachés' cipher, while Hugh Foss, another of Bletchley's great eccentrics, had broken the main Japanese diplomatic machine cipher, known to the codebreakers as the Red, in 1934 – two years before the Americans. But a new Japanese military code system introduced at the end of

1937, in which the encoded message was then enciphered to enhance its security, stumped Tiltman until the late summer of 1938. A few months later, the Japanese navy began introducing similar systems, changing its main operational code in June 1939 and cutting off the codebreakers from their main source of intelligence on the Imperial Japanese Navy. Tiltman looked at the cipher and immediately recognized it as being a similar system to the new enciphered military codes. In a typically brilliant piece of codebreaking, he managed to break the system within weeks, although it would take much longer to build up the codebook itself, which was done by British codebreakers based in Singapore. The Japanese, clearly changing all their main ciphers in preparation for war, introduced a new diplomatic machine cipher, known to the codebreakers as Purple, in early 1939, but the combination of the military attachés' cipher

and messages sent on the Red machine allowed the British codebreakers to keep on top of most Japanese diplomatic messages until February 1941, when the Americans, who had broken Purple, passed a replica of the machine to the British as part of the intelligence exchange that gave them details of the Enigma ciphers.

MI6 was still struggling with a lack of networks and productive agents, leading to scathing criticism from military officers. As late as January 1941, Air Chief Marshal Sir Robert Brooke-Popham, the British commander-in-chief in the Far East, was complaining of the poor quality of British intelligence in the region. "Weakest link undoubtedly is SIS organisation. At present little or no reliance is placed upon SIS organisation by any authorities here and little valuable information in fact appears to be obtained. I am satisfied that identity of principal officers at Shanghai, Hong Kong and Singapore is known to many. Their chief subordinates are in general local amateurs with

no training in intelligence techniques nor adequate knowledge of military, naval, air or political affairs."

One MI6 officer who served in the Tokyo embassy in 1940 reported back to London that the Japanese security police had given him "a fairly detailed outline of our SIS [Secret Intelligence Service] work in China". Stewart Menzies, the wartime chief of MI6, appointed a former MI6 representative in the region, Godfrey Denham, to be regional controller. But it was too late.

While the codebreakers could paper over the cracks in the inadequate MI6 reporting on Japanese naval and military operations, the same could not be said of intelligence on the Japanese air force, a failing which led to a disastrous underestimation of its advances in terms of aircraft capability. This and the concentration in the United Kingdom on the war with Germany led to inadequate numbers of aircraft being based in Malaya ahead of the Japanese invasion in December

1941. As a result, the Japanese completely controlled the skies over the Malay Peninsula, ensuring a swift advance south, the devastating loss of one of the Royal Navy's latest battleships, the *Prince of Wales*, and ultimately leading to the humiliatingly scrambled British withdrawal from Singapore in February 1942.

MI6 operations retreated to Delhi, where Denham failed to improve relations with the military. He was recalled to London in mid-1942 to be replaced by Leo Steveni, who had previously served with MI6 in Russia, Persia and India before being put in charge of Far Eastern intelligence at MI6 headquarters in London. Once in India, Steveni built up the MI6 operation into

ABOVE Wilfred Noyce, who worked at the British codebreaking outpost in Delhi and broke the Japanese Water Transport Code.

RIGHT British signals intelligence operators stop for a meal while collecting intelligence during the British advance through Burma.

a much larger organization known, like its Cairo equivalent, as the Inter-Services Liaison Department (ISLD). In what was probably an attempt to end the military's criticism, Steveni clearly got too close to them, following up intelligence schemes they suggested rather than taking the advice of the MI6 officers with experience on the ground.

Reports from the codebreakers, who had moved from Singapore first to Colombo in Sri Lanka and then to Mombasa in Kenya before returning to Colombo as Japanese control of the Indian Ocean ebbed and flowed, dominated British intelligence's contribution to the war in the Far East. It was not until the beginning of 1944, when Steveni was replaced by Brigadier Philip Bowden-Smith, that things began to improve, not it has to be said as a result of the activities of Bowden-Smith, a cavalry officer with no experience in intelligence whose recruitment in his club represented what was probably the worst aspect of pre-war MI6, the belief that London's clubs were the main source

of good intelligence officers. The improvement came as the result of the appointment of naval captain Gerald Garnons-Williams as head of a new MI6-controlled organization to liaise with the military. From then on, as a direct result of his activities, agents were successfully parachuted into Burma, giving considerable assistance to Allied commanders, and a number of highly productive coast-watching networks were set up along the southern Chinese coast. Meanwhile, ISLD began to leave as much frontline intelligence gathering as possible to the Special Operations Executive agents, and concentrated on setting up agent networks across the region to ensure it was not as poorly prepared for the Cold War as it had been for Japan's entry into the Second World War.

LEFT Hugh Foss, who broke the pre-war Japanese diplomatic and naval attaché cipher machines.

JOHN TILTMAN

(1894–1982)

John Tiltman (right) was one of the leading wartime codebreakers at Bletchley Park. Born in 1894, he was so brilliant as a child that at the remarkably young age of 13 he was offered a place at Oxford. He was head of the military section of the Government Code & Cipher School between the wars, breaking the ciphers of Soviet agents subverting the West. From 1935 onwards, he worked on Japanese ciphers, learning Japanese the hard way. But it was during the Second World War that his work on Japanese ciphers came into its own, with critical breaks into the main Japanese army and navy codes and ciphers. He also did important work on the German teleprinter ciphers. After the war, Tiltman stayed with the newly formed Government Communications Headquarters (GCHQ). He was appointed OBE in 1930 and CBE in 1944. He was awarded the US Legion of Merit in 1946 and appointed Commander of the Order of St Michael and St George in 1954. So critical were his codebreaking capabilities that he was retained by GCHQ until he was 70, and then went to its US counterpart, the National Security Agency, to advise a new generation of codebreakers on how to break the more difficult codes and ciphers.

RIGHT A rare Bletchley Park decrypt of an Imperial Japanese Navy movement report sent using the JN25 "super-enciphered" code system.

MOST SECRET

J.N.25C/13

June 06/130/1942   16.1 Mc/s   T.o.r. 0932

III   55/
JapSo 9915

```
         To:-  TU WI 904   -
F/I. @   MI YO RE     1st Sect. Naval Staff Imp: HQ
         I NU 804      Comb. Flt exclud: Subs.
         HI TI SO
From:    MA RA KI      C. of S. KURE Nav: Dist.
         MEDINISARI-KERAMA [?]
```

TEXT:-   Army Transport convoys (ships largely empty) leaving

Japan for the south and desiring special escort as follows:-

Leaving on 10th July for BATAVIA

ZENYOO MARU JKOL, KINUGAWA (鬼怒川) MARU JURM,
SHINNOGAWA (信濃) MARU JBTI, KANSAI (關西) MARU JEZO,
NAKO (邦古) MARU JRWZ. Speed of convoy about 13 knots. Leaving on
17th July for SINGAPORE SENKOSAN (淺香山) MARU JTNL, SOBO (本日木臭) MARU
JWUN, HIROGAWA (宏川) MARU JJFO. Speed of convoy about 14 knots.
AKIURA (昭浦) MARU JMKM (for SAIGON), YAMABUKI (山吹) MARU JCOM
(for [blank]). Speed of convoy 12.5 [knots].

SOE IN THE FAR EAST

When Japan invaded northern Malaya in December 1941, the Special Operations Executive sent stay-behind units into the jungle to work with the anti-Japanese guerrillas of the Malayan Communist Party (MCP), who had offered their services to the British government before the invasion.

There were 45 SOE soldiers organized into eight stay-behind units. They included Freddie Spencer Chapman, who harassed the Japanese during the early part of the occupation, destroying seven trains, 15 bridges and a large number of vehicles. But he lost all his team either in action or to sickness and lived with the communists for more than 18 months, out of contact with SOE headquarters in India.

SOE in the Far East was commanded by Colin Mackenzie. A Scottish textile manufacturer before the war, Mackenzie had been given a secret commission as a major-general and sent to India to coordinate special operations from Burma, across Southeast Asia and into China. He was an inspirational leader, with one SOE report noting the respect all of his men throughout Southeast Asia had "for his judgement; the faith they have in his capacity to produce the right solution for all problems; and the personal affection in which he is held". Amid near panic over a possible Japanese invasion of India, SOE spent the early part of 1942 training Indian communists as stay-behind agents, on the basis that the communists had formed the most effective resistance forces in Malaya.

John Davis, a former Malayan police officer, and Richard Broome, a former colonial-office civil servant, both of whom had been involved in the original arming of the MCP, were sent into the Malayan jungle in the summer of 1943 to find Chapman. But all three again lost contact with Delhi and it was not until early 1945, following a long trek through the jungle disguised as Chinese coolies, that they managed to escape by submarine.

Another SOE officer, Major Peter Dobrée, and his team were infiltrated into northern Malaya by parachute in December 1944, having failed to get in on two previous attempts. He landed in a blind drop, meaning that no one had prepared the landing site, so Japanese soldiers might well have coincidentally found him. One of Dobrée's agents, Ibrahim bin Ismail, had been captured by the Japanese in one of the two failed attempts. Ibrahim pretended to agree to work with his Japanese captors to draw more SOE agents into a trap: he agreed to send messages back to the Delhi headquarters of SOE, which was now known as Force 136, but omitted the security check, thereby warning Force 136 that he had been captured. The Japanese were very keen to use him to gather intelligence, making it easy for Force 136 to feed false information about British plans to the Japanese via Ibrahim in a successful deception operation. Dobrée's mission was to establish a resistance movement in northern Malaya. He set about recruiting agents to gather intelligence on Japanese forces around Taiping and in Kedah across the interstate border. By the end of March 1945, he had recruited, armed and trained 100 Malays and 80 Chinese volunteers. He also arranged the reception of four other Force 136 teams which landed by parachute, providing them with guides. The Japanese found Dobrée's jungle base in April 1945, but he and his resistance fighters managed to regroup at an alternative base and by the end of the war, he was running 300 agents gathering intelligence across northern Malaya.

Force 136 moved to Kandy in December 1944 to be close to the headquarters of South East Asia Command. It also ran agents into Burma, Thailand, French Indochina and China, and faced a much more bitter rivalry with its US equivalent, the Office for Strategic Services (OSS), in all four countries than in Europe. In China this was perhaps unsurprising since,

ABOVE SOE mess at Sosiso in Burma where Karen guerrillas were trained to operate against the Japanese.

LEFT Freddie Spencer Chapman, stayed behind the Japanese lines in Malaya after the 1941 invasion carrying out sabotage operations.

from 1943, SOE was supposed to leave operations there to the OSS.

The British Army Aid Group (BAAG), under Lieutenant-Colonel Lindsay "Blue" Ride, combined SOE operations with intelligence operations. It also helped Allied prisoners of war escape and interrogated Japanese prisoners. BAAG operated in the territory around Hong Kong that was controlled by Mao Zedong's Communist Party of China and taught the communist guerrillas of Mao's Eighth Route Army special operations techniques developed during operations alongside the resistance in Europe. Ride's mission had to be kept completely secret, since it not only breached the agreement between SOE and the Americans but would also have provoked a furious reaction from the nationalist Chinese leader Chiang Kai-shek, who was working closely with Findlay Andrew, the SOE representative in the nationalist capital of Chungking.

A third mission inside China mounted two operations, Remorse and Waldorf, which focused entirely on making money from the black market. It was run by Walter Fletcher, a former businessman described by one of his fellow SOE officers as "a thug with good commercial contacts", who made

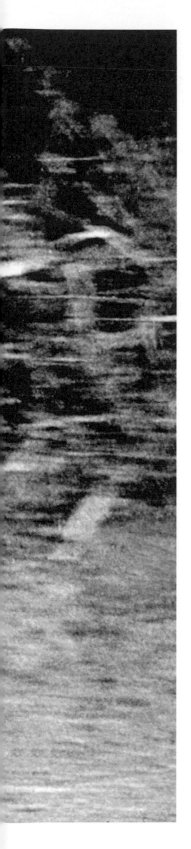

ABOVE Peter Fleming, brother of James Bond author Ian Fleming, mounted deception operations against the Japanese in Burma.

LEFT A Chinese soldier fighting with the British runs through the Burmese jungle.

some £77m ($310m) by dealing in a variety of goods from rubber to quinine and dealing on the black-market currency exchanges. Fletcher made money on almost everything he traded in, which also included machinery, diamonds and at one point Chinese silkworms. The money more than covered the cost of SOE operations across Southeast Asia.

An SOE plan to mount a coup d'état in Thailand that might have made the 1941 Japanese invasion more difficult was turned down, and thereafter SOE operations there focused on supporting the Free Thai Movement, which provided valuable intelligence from inside Thailand, and working with Luang Pridi, the prince regent, to help him persuade the Japanese to relax their hold on the country.

The British mounted very few special operations in French Indochina (now Vietnam, Laos and Cambodia), where the Americans were funding, supplying and building up the communist Viet Minh, under Ho Chi Minh, into a formidable force that entirely controlled the north of the country, much to America's subsequent regret.

By the time the war came to an end, in August 1945, Force 136 had grown to such an extent that it was running more than 30,000 agents across Southeast Asia.

FORCE 136 IN BURMA

Burma was the main theatre of war for British forces in southeast Asia and the SOE played a key role. The British had particularly strong links with the Karen people who lived in the mountains bordering Thailand. Large numbers of them joined the Burma Rifles and when the Japanese invaded forcing the British retreat to India, many of them were given three months pay and told to take their rifle and ammunition back to their home villages, providing ready-made stay-behind units. A number of Burma Rifles officers stayed with them to organise the resistance. It took more than a year before they were reinforced with other agents and wireless operators. Major Hugh Seagrim, one of the British officers, was the subject of an intensive search by the Japanese in late 1943 and early 1944 to track him down. He eventually gave himself up to stop the Japanese reprisals against Karen villages and was executed with eight of his men. Seagrim was posthumously awarded the George Cross. The Karen continued to fight the Japanese, organizing around 10,000 fighters who staged an uprising in April 1945 which prevented the Japanese troops from blocking the Allied advance on Rangoon. They are estimated to have killed some 17,000 Japanese troops.

SPECIAL FORCES IN THE SECOND WORLD WAR

There were a number of British special forces units working across a variety of theatres during the Second World War, all of which eventually fed into two main units, the British Army's Special Air Service (SAS) and the Royal Navy's Special Boat Squadron (SBS), now the Special Boat Service.

The Special Boat Section was originally formed in July 1940 by a Royal Marine Commando officer, Roger "Jumbo" Courtney. It was originally known as the Folboat Troop because of the folding canoes it used in raiding operations. The SBS worked initially with Layforce, a Royal Marine Commando unit commanded by Lieutenant-Colonel Robert Laycock, which was formed in February 1941 to carry out coastal raids and collect intelligence in the Middle East. Its intelligence officer was the author Evelyn Waugh. A second Special Boat Section was formed in December 1941, although 1st SBS subsequently lost a number of its men, including all but two of a 10-man team during a raid on Rhodes in September 1942, and was briefly absorbed into the SAS. It was reformed in April 1943 as the Special Boat Squadron, making more than 400 raids across the Greek islands and into Albania and Yugoslavia. Meanwhile, 2nd Special Boat Section, retaining the original name, took part in the "Torch" North Africa landings of November 1942 and the Salerno Landings the following September, before moving to the Far East and operating along the Chindwin and Irrawaddy rivers during the Burma Campaign.

TOP Colonel Vladimir Peniakoff (centre) set up the a special operations force known as Popski's Private Army to mount raids in North Africa.

ABOVE Major Herbert Hasler and Corporal Bill Sparks (right), the sole surviving Cockleshell Heroes, with Mary Lindell, who helped them escape.

ABOVE The author Evelyn Waugh was intelligence officer for the Special Boat Section and influential in the creation of the Special Air Service.

LEFT General Orde Wingate (centre) with Chindit officers, including Brigadier Mike Calvert (second from left).

The Special Boat Service also traces its origins back to the Combined Operations Pilotage Parties, a deliberately deceptive name for a unit which carried out harbour and beach reconnaissance ahead of the Allied landings in Italy and France, and to the original "Cockleshell Heroes", the members of the Royal Marines Boom Patrol Detachment formed in July 1942 by Major H G "Blondie" Hasler. Their heroic title derives from the "Cockle" canoes they used during their most famous action on 11 December 1942, when a 10-man team led by Hasler paddled up the Gironde estuary to Bordeaux to plant mines on German blockade-running merchantmen. Eight of the 10 canoeists were drowned or shot and only Hasler and Marine Bill Sparks survived.

The first of the British Army units from which the SAS is descended was arguably the Long Range Desert Group (LRDG), which was formed in May 1940 by Captain Ralph Bagnold to mount operations behind enemy lines in North Africa. These included not only the insertion of MI6 agents, but also collecting intelligence themselves and mounting surprise raids on enemy fuel and supply dumps. They operated in specially adapted trucks and jeeps designed to cope with the difficulties of off-road driving in the desert, in which they became expert survivors. The most important intelligence they provided was reconnaissance ahead of Montgomery's advances and confirmation of intelligence already collected by Bletchley Park and by mobile army intercept units operating in the desert. This not only validated the codebreakers' intelligence, but by skilful use of evidence of the LRDG's presence – through the killing of sentries on outer perimeters, for example – explained how the Allies had acquired the intelligence and therefore helped to prevent the Germans realizing that the Enigma ciphers had been broken. The LRDG subsequently moved to operations in the Adriatic and the Greek islands, where it was less effective, and ultimately in early 1944 to take part in the final push for control of Rome and northern Italy.

Perhaps the most colourful of the predecessors of the SAS was Popski's Private Army, which was set up by a former LRDG member, Vladimir Peniakoff, a Belgian émigré of Russian extraction who had been nicknamed "Popski" while serving with the LRDG. Officially designated No 1 Demolition Squadron, Popski's Private Army operated in armed jeeps behind enemy lines in North Africa alongside the LRDG and carried out raids on enemy airfields, destroying aircraft and vehicles. When the invasion of Italy began in September 1943, it moved there, again operating behind enemy lines, but this time fighting with the Partisans much in the manner of the SOE.

The Special Air Service proper was formed by David Stirling in October 1941, initially using former members of Layforce (of

LEFT British explorer Wilfred Thesiger, an early recruit into the Special Air Service operating behind enemy lines in North Africa.

OPPOSITE The Long Range Desert Group, formed in May 1940, which operated behind enemy lines and was the predecessor of the SAS.

which he had been a part). Stirling was an unlikely creator of the SAS. Although his uncle had formed the Lovat Scouts during the Boer War, describing them as "half wolf, half jack-rabbit", Stirling was not regarded as the most responsible of officers. He had a reputation for drinking, gambling and partying. The SAS also operated originally in the Middle East and formed raiding parties which were inserted and extracted by the LRDG to mount raids on German rear echelon forces. The title itself came from a deception operation mounted by British intelligence in the Middle East which created a fictitious unit called 1st Special Air Service Brigade in order to suggest there was a large British airborne force based in Cairo. Stirling's new team was made part of that unit as L Detachment, the Special Air Service, and included in its number the explorer and writer Wilfred Thesiger. The combination of the LRDG and the SAS was extraordinarily effective. One of Stirling's men, Lieutenant Robert "Paddy" Mayne, described by one of his fellow officers as "an extremely truculent Irishman when he is drink taken", destroyed 37 aircraft in a single night, with no evidence of any "drink taken". In September 1942, Stirling's unit became 1st SAS Regiment and a second regiment, commanded by Stirling's brother Bill, was formed in early 1943.

But in January 1943 Stirling was captured during an operation in Tunisia and 1st SAS was dissolved, while its remaining members were formed into the Special Raiding Squadron which operated in Italy alongside 2nd SAS, retaining the SAS insignia and beret. Both units returned to the UK in early 1944, with the SRS becoming 1st SAS again and both regiments joining with a Belgian SAS squadron, two French SAS regiments and the Phantom Regiment (a special forces intelligence unit) to form 1st SAS Brigade, which fought during the Normandy landings, in Belgium and Holland and into Germany before being disbanded in October 1945.

One other special forces unit should not be forgotten. Brigadier Orde Wingate formed Long-Range Penetration groups to fight behind Japanese lines in Burma in June 1942. They came to be known as the Chindits, named after the *chinthay*, mythical creatures which guarded Buddhist temples in the jungles of Southeast Asia. There were doubts over the effectiveness of Wingate's forces, but these were not shared by Mike Calvert, one of his senior officers, who was a prime mover behind the regeneration of the SAS in Malaya in the early 1950s.

ANDERS LASSEN – "THE GREAT DANE"
(1920–1945)

One of the most astonishingly brave members of the British special forces during the Second World War was a Dane. Anders Lassen left Denmark shortly after the start of the war, joining the British Army's Small Scale Raiding Force as a private. He was commissioned in the field and awarded the Military Cross for bravery during a raid on Axis shipping off West Africa in January 1942. His unit was subsequently absorbed into the SAS, in which he was promoted to captain and then to major, collecting two additional bars to his Military Cross in the process. But even this extraordinary feat would be bettered during an operation in Italy in April 1945, when Lassen, now just 24 years of age and already an officer commanding the Special Boat Squadron, took part in a raid on the northern shore of Lake Comacchio. Lassen and his men were attacked by the German defenders. He personally overran three enemy positions, removing six machine-guns and a dozen German soldiers from the battle, before being mortally wounded by machine-gun fire. Displaying what the citation for his Victoria Cross described as "magnificent courage", Lassen refused to be evacuated, dying where he lay, rather than risk the lives of his men.

INTELLIGENCE FOR D-DAY

The first half of 1944 was dominated by preparations for D-Day, the planned Allied invasion of France. One of the key areas of interest was the German defences across the northern French coastline, which formed part of the Atlantic Wall, the so-called *Festung Europa* or "Fortress Europe", which ran from northern Norway down to the northern border between France and Spain.

Bletchley Park was unable to intercept the communications of the German defensive posts along the French Channel coast because most ran via landline, but fortunately various Japanese officials were given extensive guided tours of the defences and sent detailed accounts back to Tokyo in various different ciphers, thus ensuring the codebreakers could give the D-Day planners its entire layout.

Among the more important diplomatic intercepts in the run-up to D-Day was a detailed report on the German defences in northern France by General Hiroshi Oshima, the Japanese ambassador in Berlin, based on a tour he made in November 1943. His report was sent to Tokyo using the Japanese high-grade diplomatic machine cipher, a code that had been broken by the United States codebreakers. One of the Americans working on the Purple messages later recalled the excitement of working through the night and into the next day on Oshima's detailed rundown of the French portion of the Atlantic Wall. "I was too electrified to sleep," he said. "In the end we produced what was a veritable pamphlet, an on-the-ground description of the north French defences of *Festung Europa*, composed *dictu mirabile* by a general."

The gaps in Oshima's report were more than filled in by Colonel Ito Seiichi, the Japanese military attaché, who had made his own tour of the entire German coastal defences, sending a massive 32-part report back to Tokyo in the Japanese military attaché cipher that had been broken by John Tiltman. The reports reassured the Allies that Hitler remained convinced that the main thrust of the invasion was to be along the Pas de Calais, a key issue in the Allied planning.

In early May, the Japanese naval attaché in Berlin made his own tour of the German defences. Sent on the Coral machine in the newly broken JNA20 cipher, his report was easily read by the Allies. It was more authoritative than that of Oshima, whose pro-German tendencies led him to accept unquestioningly what he was told. Rommel, who had been appointed to lead the main force resisting an invasion, intended "to destroy the enemy near the coast, most of all on the beaches, without allowing them to penetrate any considerable distance inland," the naval attaché said. "As defence against airborne operations

OPPOSITE Members of the French resistance collected intelligence on the German defences and destroyed 1800 trains in the two months before D-Day.

BELOW Japanese ambassador in Berlin Hiroshi Oshima, whose detailed reports of Germany's defences in France were read at Bletchley Park.

THE COLOSSUS COMPUTER

Colossus was the world's first programmable, digital, electronic computer. It was developed to help the Bletchley Park codebreakers decipher the high-grade German messages sent using the SZ42 Schlüsselzusatz enciphered teleprinter (the "Tunny"). Alan Turing's only involvement in the construction of Colossus was to recommend that Tommy Flowers, a post office engineer, should be consulted on problems with an earlier unreliable machine known as Heath Robinson. Max Newman, a mathematician and codebreaker, believed computers could be used to break Tunny. Flowers persuaded Newman that a fully electronic machine using vacuum tubes would solve the problems and then built it himself. Neither Heath Robinson nor Colossus actually deciphered the messages; they provided information that allowed the codebreakers to break into them. Eleven Colossus computers were built and all but two were destroyed at the end of the war. The intense secrecy surrounding the existence of Colossus led to the American ENIAC machine, which was not operational until July 1946, being claimed erroneously as the world's first programmable digital electronic computer.

he plans to cut communications between seaborne and airborne troops and to destroy them individually." The report gave detailed appraisals of the German dispositions and intentions and, worryingly for the Allies, said Normandy was regarded as a prime target for the Allies and was being reinforced. This trend was confirmed by a report from Oshima of a meeting with Hitler at which the Führer had told him that the British were expected to establish an initial bridgehead in Normandy before launching the main front against the Pas de Calais.

But the most important ciphers remained the high-grade German ciphers. The highest-level communications between top-level German commanders and Berlin was now sent using enciphered teleprinter traffic employing the SZ42 Schlüsselzusatz. Bletchley Park called enciphered teleprinter communications Fish and gave individual systems codenames based on different types of fish; the SZ42 was known as Tunny. Initially, it was broken by hand at Bletchley but Max Newman, one of the

RIGHT The SZ42 Schlüsselzusatz enciphered high-grade German teleprinter traffic; its output was deciphered using the Colossus computer.

mathematicians breaking Tunny, believed that, using principles first laid down by Alan Turing in his pre-war treatise "On Computable Numbers", a computing machine could be devised which would make their difficult task very much easier. Newman put forward a plan to create the computer and Charles Eryll Wynn-Williams of the Telecommunications Research Establishment, who was based at Malvern in Worcestershire and had worked on the high-speed Bombes, was called in try to create it. The first machine, known at Bletchley Park as Heath Robinson, into which the teleprinter tape from the intercepted traffic was fed, was able to compare the enciphered message to the SZ42's wheel patterns, but it was labour-intensive and unreliable. Next, Newman called in Tommy Flowers, a telephone engineer from the Post Office Research Station at Dollis Hill in north London, who created a new machine, known as Colossus (see opposite), which was introduced in February 1944.

Colossus allowed the codebreakers to read the main teleprinter link between Field Marshal Gerd von Rundstedt, the commander-in-chief of German forces in the West, and Berlin. This link, known as Jellyfish to the codebreakers, produced vital intelligence on German preparations to counter the Allied invasion and a complete German order of battle. It also updated the descriptions of the German defences given by the various Japanese visitors in their reports to Tokyo.

MI6 also contributed to the intelligence picture ahead of D-Day. The various French agent networks, some controlled through the Gaullist Bureau Central de Renseignements et

FOLLOWING PAGES Bletchley Park and MI6 provided detailed intelligence of the German "Atlantic Wall" defences ahead of D-Day.

FAR RIGHT General Charles de Gaulle, whose Free French Bureau Central de Renseignements et d'Action produced intelligence on the German defences in France.

d'Action, some through the Poles and some, like the large Alliance network, directly by MI6, provided extensive details of German military activity. French agents stole the plans for the Atlantic Wall and provided detailed sketches of the beaches where the landings were to take place. Other members of the Free French forces were part of Operation Sussex, a joint enterprise with the Bureau Central de Renseignements et d'Action and the American Office for Strategic Services (OSS), in which two-person French teams, including female agents, were trained by MI6 before being dropped into Normandy to provide up-to-date tactical intelligence. A total of 20 teams were sent in to provide detailed intelligence on 50 separate targets in the areas the Allied forces were attacking. Ahead of the actual Normandy landings themselves, which began on 6 June, RAF reconnaissance aircraft repeatedly flew over the northern French coast providing confirmation of the locations logged from the Japanese intercepts of the German defences, and special forces "pilotage parties" carried out reconnaissance of the Normandy beaches, getting close inshore on board mini-submarines.

OPERATION FORTITUDE SOUTH – THE D-DAY DECEPTION

Churchill was as fascinated with deception operations as he was with espionage. At the Teheran Conference in November 1943, when the final decision was made to launch the invasion of Europe in mid-1944, the British Prime Minister told Stalin that "in wartime, truth is so precious that she should always be attended by a bodyguard of lies".

From that point on, the overall deception plan for D-Day was known as Operation Bodyguard. The double-agent handlers now had to think continuously about the various elements of the deception plan and how the agents could be used to convince the Germans they were true. The Double Cross system became like a game of chess, with the agents resembling pieces, each being carefully moved into a position where it could contribute to the opponent's demise.

The key element of Fortitude South, the deception plan to cover the actual D-Day landings, was that the Germans should be led to believe that the Normandy landings were a feint aimed at drawing German forces away from the main thrust of the Allied invasion, which would be directed against the Pas de Calais. This would ensure that the bulk of the German forces would be held back from the Normandy beaches, allowing the Allies time to establish a strong foothold in northern France from which they could break out towards Paris and then on to the German border.

A completely mythical formation, the First United States Army Group (FUSAG), was invented, supposedly commanded by General George Patton, a hero of the invasion of Sicily and a man whom the Germans would believe must be heavily involved in the invasion of Europe. FUSAG was supposedly grouped in East Anglia and southeast England, and it was vital that the agents' reports were coordinated to show that this was the case, and to downplay the mass of troops waiting in the south and southwest to attack the German defences in Normandy.

The most spectacularly useful of the double agents used in the Fortitude South deception plan was Garbo (see page 145). Among the other agents who, in the parlance of the Twenty Committee, "came up for D-Day", the most important was the triple agent Brutus. Roman Garby-Czerniawski, a Pole, had led the Interallié agent network in France and, once it was uncovered, volunteered to work for the Abwehr in London in order to save his fellow agents from execution. On arrival in Britain, he immediately told the authorities of his mission and was turned against the Germans. Two others were also important to Fortitude South: Tricycle and Nathalie "Lily"

RIGHT A German chart of false British unit insignia fed to the Abwehr by Garbo and the other double agents.

Sergueiew (Treasure), a French citizen born in Russia whose family had fled in the wake of the Bolshevik revolution.

All four of these helped in building up Fortitude South, the false picture of the intended target of D-Day. Tricycle and Brutus, who was supposedly a member of a Polish unit attached to FUSAG, provided an order of battle for the fictitious formation so detailed that the Germans were supplied not just with information on individual units, strengths and locations, but even with reproductions of the insignia painted on the side of their vehicles. Treasure's role was to report from the West Country that there were very few troops there, further pushing the Germans towards the view that the main thrust of the attack would be against the Pas de Calais. But by far the most important and complex role was played by Garbo.

The German belief in the existence of FUSAG was steadily built up by a number of means, apart from the false reports from

OPPOSITE Nathalie "Lily" Sergueiew (codename Treasure), a French citizen born in Russia, was key to the D-Day deception.

BELOW Allied troops landing on the Normandy beaches. Without the D-Day deception they might never have managed to get ashore.

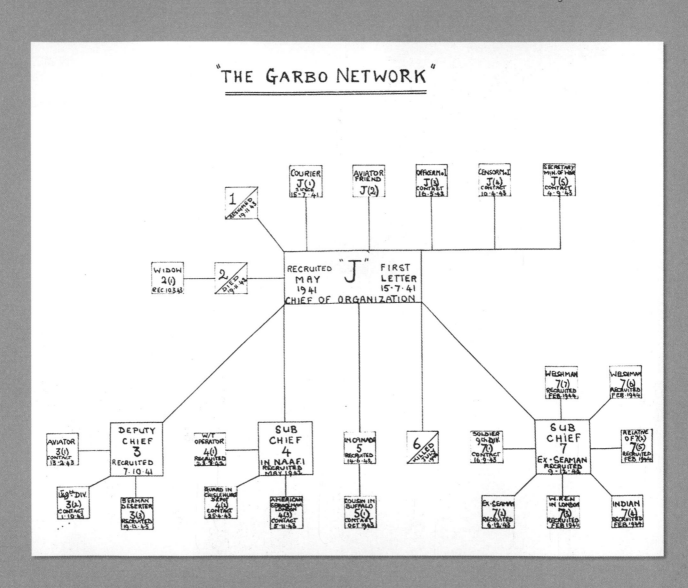

GARBO – THE MOST SUCCESSFUL DOUBLE AGENT

The most successful of the Double Cross agents was the Spaniard Juan Pujol García. He was recruited by the Abwehr to report from London, but based himself in Lisbon from where he used a Blue Guide to Britain and a book on the Royal Navy to compile a series of ludicrous reports that the Germans accepted at face value. In February 1942 he offered to work for the British as a double agent and was taken to London where, under the codename Garbo, he fed false information to the Abwehr that fitted with the Double Cross deception. At one point, Garbo's 27 agents included a Swiss businessman in Bootle reporting "drunken orgies and slack morals

in amusement centres" in Liverpool and a Venezuelan in Glasgow who claimed Clydeside dockers would "do anything for a litre of wine". When the Swiss businessman died of cancer, his widow took his place. The Venezuelan also ran agents in Scotland, one of them a communist who thought he was working for Moscow. Garbo's mistress, a secretary in the War Cabinet, slept with army officers to gather valuable pillow talk. Garbo set up a network of agents in Wales, mostly Welsh Nationalists, who were led by "a thoroughly undesirable character" who worked purely for money. It is important to remember that none of these people actually existed.

the double agents. Dummy invasion craft nicknamed "Big Bobs" were left out in the open in east-coast ports, and mobile wireless vehicles travelling around southeast England broadcast messages from a number of different locations to fool the German radio-interception units.

During the second half of May 1944, Garbo told his German controller in Madrid that he had accepted a job in the Ministry of Information which would give him access to details of all propaganda designed to cover up the invasion plans. By reading these "in reverse" he would be able to detect the real plans, he said. On 29 May, he sent a message saying that he had now studied all the propaganda directives. "What I was clearly able to get out of it and what I consider to be of maximum importance is the intention to hide the facts in order to trick us," he said. He was bringing his Venezuelan deputy down from Scotland to assist him in sending off the messages. This man could not speak German, Garbo explained, enquiring if his controllers would mind if the deputy sent his messages in English. The Germans readily agreed and the stage was set for Garbo's greatest triumph.

In the early hours of D-Day, 6 June 1944, with Allied forces pouring across the English Channel, Garbo made repeated attempts to warn his Abwehr controller that the Allies were on their way. It was too late for the Germans to do anything about it, but it ensured they still believed in Garbo as their best-informed secret agent even after the invasion had begun, and it paved the way for the next stage of the deception.

Shortly after midnight on 9 June, as the Allied advance faltered, and with the elite 1st SS Panzer division, together with another armoured division, on its way to reinforce the German defences in Normandy, Garbo sent his most important message. Three of his agents were reporting troops massed across East Anglia and Kent and large numbers of troop and tank transporters waiting in the eastern ports, he said. "After personal consultation on 8th June in London with my agents Donny, Dick and Derrick, whose reports I sent today, I am of the opinion, in view of the strong troop concentrations in southeast and east England, that these operations are a diversionary manoeuvre designed to draw off enemy reserves in order to make an attack at another place. In view of the continued air attacks on the concentration area mentioned, which is a strategically favourable position for this, it may very probably take place in the Pas de Calais area."

Garbo's warning went straight to Hitler, who ordered the two divisions back to the Pas de Calais to defend against what he expected to be the main invasion thrust. This ensured the success of the Allied invasion. Had the two divisions continued to Normandy, the Allies might well have been thrown back into the sea.

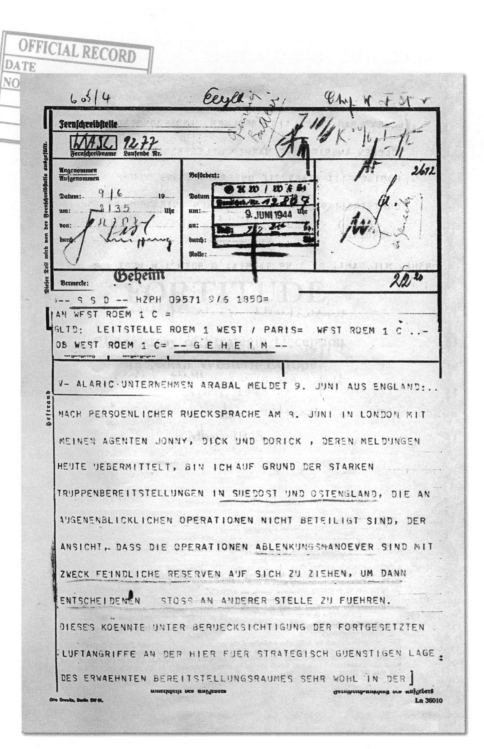

LEFT Garbo's most important message sent shortly after midnight on 9 June 1944, three days after the Normandy landings, warned of a second larger Allied invasion force heading for the Pas de Calais which forced Hitler to keep two Panzer divisions in the Calais area, ensuring the success of the Normandy landings.

TRANSLATION

TO:	West Roem 1C
FROM:	Alaric
DATE:	9. 6. '44
COMMENTS:	Secret

Alaric of the Arabal company reporting from England, 9th June:

Following personal contact in London on 8th June with my agents Jonny, Dick and Dorick (their reports passed on today), it is my opinion, based on the large-scale troop preparations in South-East England and East Anglia which are unconnected with present operations, that the operations could be diversionary tactics, carried out with the intention of inciting enemy reserves to attack them, in order to inflict a decisive blow at another location. In view of the continuous air raids on strategically favourable locations for this, the area for which preparations are being made could very probably be the Pas de Calais region, especially as if such an attack were to take place, the fact that the air support points are nearer would make such an enterprise easier.

RSHA, Mil. Amt., BR B no. 3435/A4 G Roem 1 H Woot/: V. (illegible)

(Handwritten comment) Underlines our previous opinion, in accordance with which a second blow is to be expected in another area (Belgium?)

K

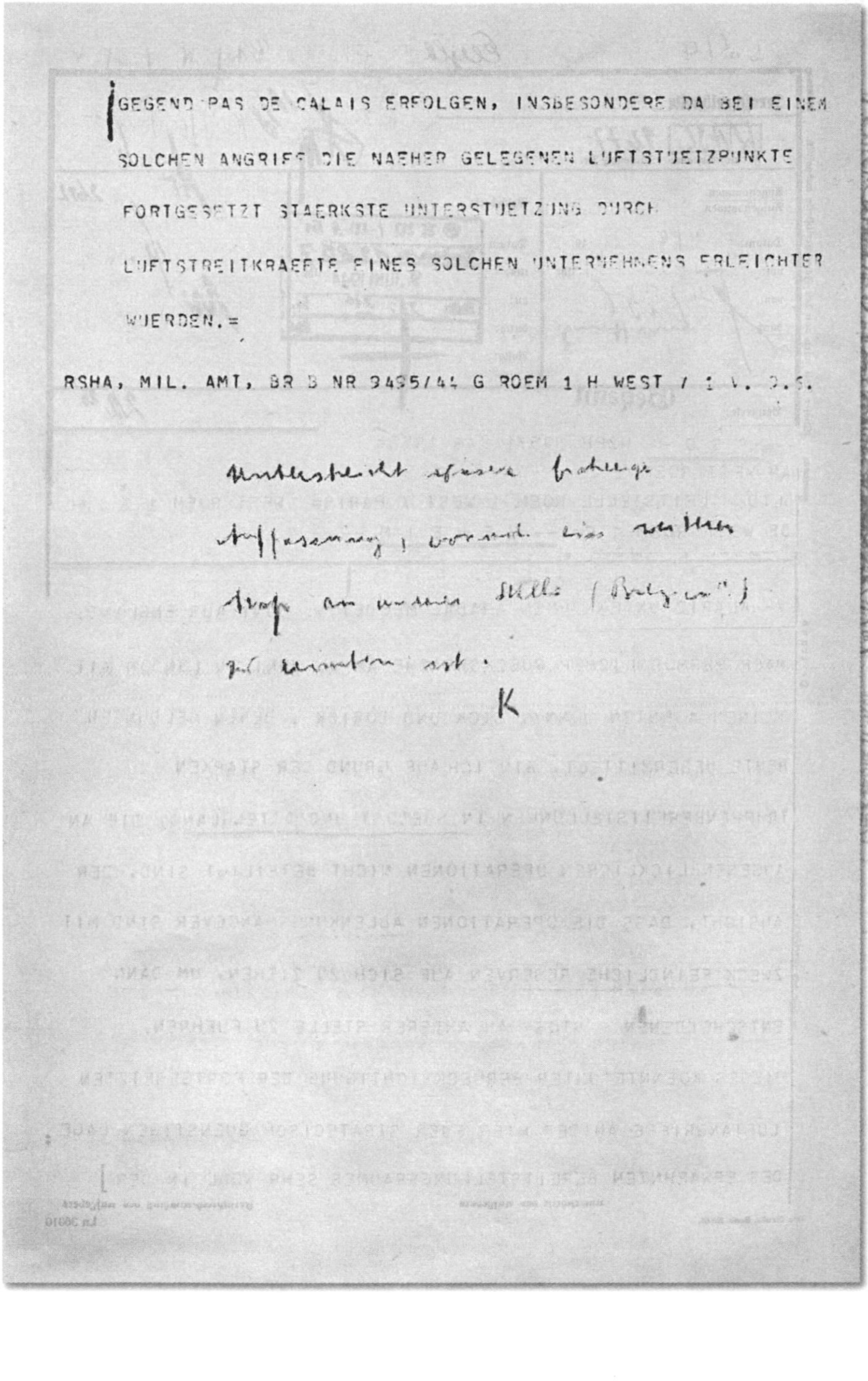
GEGEND PAS DE CALAIS ERFOLGEN, INSBESONDERE DA BEI EINEM
SOLCHEN ANGRIFF DIE NAEHER GELEGENEN LUFTSTUETZPUNKTE
FORTGESETZT STAERKSTE UNTERSTUETZUNG DURCH
LUFTSTREITKRAEFTE EINES SOLCHEN UNTERNEHMENS ERLEICHTER
WUERDEN.=

RSHA, MIL. AMT, BR B NR 3435/44 G ROEM 1 H WEST / [illegible]

Unterstreicht unsere frühere Auffassung, wonach ein weiterer Stoss an anderer Stelle (Belgien?) zu erwarten ist.

K

GERMAN INTELLIGENCE
HOW IT FARED

The main German intelligence service at the start of the war was the military intelligence service the Abwehr, run by Admiral Wilhelm Canaris. Although its name means "defence" in German, it was in fact an intelligence-collection service with extensive networks across Europe.

TOP LEFT Hans Bernd Gisevius, the Abwehr representative in Zurich, who passed intelligence to both the British and Americans.

BELOW LEFT Admiral Wilhelm Canaris, the head of German military intelligence, the Abwehr, he was arrested in 1944 on suspicion of treason and executed in April 1945.

OPPOSITE Colonel Reinhard Gehlen (centre), head of German intelligence on the Eastern Front. His knowledge of the Russians was invaluable after the war when he became head of West German intelligence.

C anaris opposed the Nazi regime, but played a very careful game, continuing to provide good intelligence to his bosses in the German High Command while deliberately feeding details of the German planning and intentions to both the British and the Americans. He passed information to the British via a Polish MI6 agent in Switzerland, Madame Halina Szymanska, to whom he was very close – it is alleged they were lovers – and through Hans-Bernd Gisevius, the Abwehr representative in Zurich, who also handed intelligence to Allen Dulles, the OSS representative in Switzerland.

The Abwehr had some notable successes, in particular Operation Nordpol (North Pole), also known as *Das Englandspiel* (England game), in which the entire SOE agent network in Holland – some 50 agents – was rounded up by the Germans and turned back against the British to feed false information, a coup masterminded by Abwehr officer Hermann Giskes. The incompetence involved on the British side which allowed this to happen – security checks were omitted from messages by the captured agents, but their absence was ignored in London and more agents sent in – has led to suggestions that the Dutch networks were deliberately given up to bolster

Canaris's position, which was becoming increasingly tenuous, although there is no concrete evidence to support the theory.

Throughout the war, Heinrich Himmler, the head of the SS, was working to displace the Abwehr as Germany's main intelligence service and replace it with the Nazi Party's own internal intelligence and security organization, the Sicherheitsdienst (Security Service), which he controlled; the process was accelerated in early 1944 following the defection of an Abwehr officer in Turkey. Canaris was not involved in the July 1944 plot to kill Hitler, but as the result of the interrogation of one of the conspirators, details of Canaris's opposition to the regime were exposed and he was imprisoned. He was hanged in April 1945.

Curiously, the man who was probably the most successful Abwehr operative was a sergeant, although Hugo Bleicher often posed as an army colonel. Bleicher was particularly efficient at tracking down SOE and MI6 networks in France. He broke up the Polish Interallié intelligence network, capturing both the leader of the network, Roman Czerniawski, and one of his key aides, Mathilde Carré, who became Bleicher's lover. Both agreed to work for the Germans, but while Carré betrayed

the network's other agents, Czerniawski went to London, ostensibly to spy for Bleicher, and immediately handed himself over to MI5, who ran him as one of the most successful of the Double Cross agents, under the codename Brutus. Carré was subsequently also persuaded to go to London and was used to feed false intelligence back to the Germans. Bleicher's other successes include infiltrating the Carte resistance network and the arrests of the SOE officer Peter Churchill and his FANY courier Odette Sansom.

The Abwehr's greatest coup was in the dismantling of the Europe-wide Soviet intelligence network known as the Rote Kapelle (Red Orchestra). The increased wireless activity between the network's agents and Moscow in the immediate aftermath of the German assault on Soviet-controlled territory in June 1941 allowed the Germans to track down a number of agent transmissions, and the first arrests took place in Brussels in December 1941; more followed swiftly, and the network's agents in Paris were rounded up, followed by those in Germany. By the end of 1942, the vast bulk of the network had been closed down. Its value to the Allied war effort was overstated as part of the post-war Soviet Bloc propaganda, but Canaris estimated that it must have led to the deaths of 200,000 Germans.

There were a number of different German organizations intercepting and breaking British, American and Russian codes and ciphers, the most notable of which were the German army's Horchdienst (Listening Service), the naval Beobachtungsdienst (Observation Service), generally known as the B-Dienst, and the German High Command's Entzifferungsdienst (Deciphering Service) or E-Dienst. At the start of the war, the Horchdienst had 10 static stations in Germany and eight mobile Horchkompanien (Listening Companies) attached to the major command headquarters. The Horchkompanien were an integral part of the Wehrmacht's Blitzkrieg warfare system and the most important German source for enemy order of battle assessments.

The B-Dienst broke the Royal Navy's Administrative Code, the most widely used of the Royal Navy's codes, several years before the war, allowing it to concentrate on the Naval Cypher No 1, which was used by officers for more sensitive messages. The full extent of its early successes became clear in April 1940 during the short-lived British response to the German invasion of Norway, by which time the B-Dienst was reading between 30 and 50 per cent of the Royal Navy messages it intercepted. This resulted in changes to both the Royal Navy Administrative Code and the Naval Cypher. But by September 1941, the B-Dienst was breaking the new Naval Cypher No 2 extensively, and even the introduction of the new Naval Cypher No 4 in January 1942 only slowed it down slightly. By October 1942, it was having increasing success against No 4. The Naval Cypher No 3, which was used by Royal Navy escorts on Atlantic convoys to communicate with Canadian and US allies, proved even more vulnerable. It was introduced in June 1941, and by February 1942 the Germans were reading around 80 per cent of the messages, often giving them 20 hours' notice of convoy routes and allowing U-Boat wolf packs to line up in ambush formation. When Bletchley Park finally broke into the Shark Enigma cipher at the end of 1942, this vulnerability became apparent and both the No 3 and No 4 Cyphers were changed to a more secure system that the B-Dienst was unable to break.

The Germans never succeeded in breaking the British equivalent of the Enigma cipher, the Typex cipher machine, which was in fact originally based on Enigma but incorporated security measures developed by the British as a result of their knowledge of where Enigma had proved vulnerable. They did, however, have remarkable success against highly complex Soviet enciphered teleprinter systems.

RIGHT Hugo Bleicher, the highly successful Abwehr sergeant who arrested more SOE and MI6 agents than any other German intelligence officer.

BELOW Gestapo officers posing in front of their Paris headquarters. The officer fourth from right in the second row (circled) is Paul Thümmel, who was spying for MI6 via Czech intelligence.

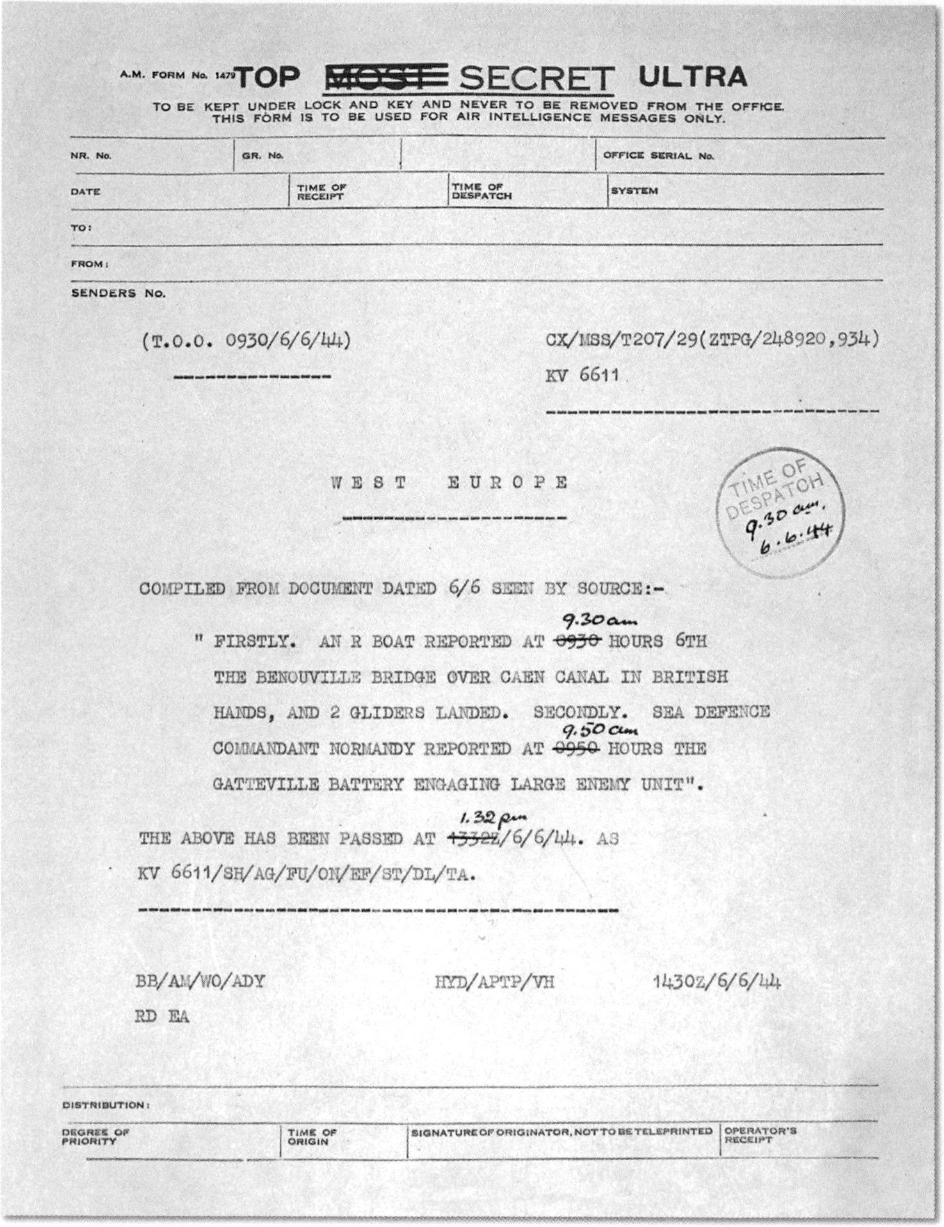

A.M. FORM No. 1479 **TOP** ~~MOST~~ **SECRET ULTRA**

TO BE KEPT UNDER LOCK AND KEY AND NEVER TO BE REMOVED FROM THE OFFICE.
THIS FORM IS TO BE USED FOR AIR INTELLIGENCE MESSAGES ONLY.

NR. No.		GR. No.			OFFICE SERIAL No.
DATE		TIME OF RECEIPT	TIME OF DESPATCH		SYSTEM
TO:					
FROM:					

SENDERS No.

(T.O.O. 0930/6/6/44)   CX/MSS/T207/29(ZTPG/248920,934)

————————   KV 6611

————————————————————

WEST   EUROPE

————————

TIME OF DESPATCH 9.30 am. 6.6.44

COMPILED FROM DOCUMENT DATED 6/6 SEEN BY SOURCE:-

     9.30 am

" FIRSTLY. AN R BOAT REPORTED AT ~~0930~~ HOURS 6TH

THE BENOUVILLE BRIDGE OVER CAEN CANAL IN BRITISH

HANDS, AND 2 GLIDERS LANDED.   SECONDLY.   SEA DEFENCE

     9.50 am

COMMANDANT NORMANDY REPORTED AT ~~0950~~ HOURS THE

GATTEVILLE BATTERY ENGAGING LARGE ENEMY UNIT".

    1.32 pm

THE ABOVE HAS BEEN PASSED AT ~~1332~~Z/6/6/44. AS

KV 6611/SH/AG/FU/ON/EF/ST/DL/TA.

————————————————————

BB/AM/WO/ADY   HYD/APTP/VH   1430Z/6/6/44

RD EA

| DISTRIBUTION: | | | | |
| DEGREE OF PRIORITY | TIME OF ORIGIN | SIGNATURE OF ORIGINATOR, NOT TO BE TELEPRINTED | OPERATOR'S RECEIPT |

LEFT A German D-Day report, deciphered at Bletchley Park, reporting that British airborne forces had captured a bridge over the Caen Canal and that coastal batteries were engaging a large Allied force. The report is written up to look as if it came from an agent in order to protect the Enigma secret.

ABOVE The British Typex cipher machine, based on the workings of the Enigma machine but with amendments to increase its security.

PREPARING FOR "THE NEXT WAR"

Long before the end of the war, British intelligence was preparing for a future war in which Russia was expected to be the main enemy. Operation Barbarossa – the German invasion of the Soviet Union – began on 22 June 1941.

According to the official history of British Intelligence in the Second World War, at that point all intelligence operations against the Soviet Union came to an abrupt halt on the orders of Britain's Prime Minister Winston Churchill. In fact, if anything, the effort by the British codebreakers initially increased and it was not until December 1941 that the GC&CS operation to break Russian codes and ciphers was shut down.

But this did not mean that the Russian military and naval traffic was no longer being intercepted in the United Kingdom and that its codes and ciphers were no longer being broken. The Polish codebreakers who escaped from Eastern Europe went first to France and then some of them came to the United Kingdom. But they could not be allowed to go to Bletchley Park to work on Enigma ciphers or to know the progress the British codebreakers had made, because they had families still living behind enemy lines and were therefore vulnerable to blackmail.

Since the main threats to Poland in the pre-war period had been Germany to the west and Russia to the east, the Polish codebreakers were also experts in Russian codes and ciphers. So they set up a Russian codebreaking section at Stanmore in Middlesex, and in June 1941 were asked by MI6 not to stop their work but to throw more resources into it.

There is some evidence to suggest that Dilly Knox, the Bletchley Park chief cryptographer, who by the end of 1941 was dying of cancer, spent the remaining 14 months of his life working at home trying to break Soviet ciphers, assisted only by a female codebreaker, Margaret Rock. But Knox died in February 1943 and by July of that year, when the Polish codebreakers had moved to Boxmoor, 26 kilometres (16 miles) north of Stanmore, they remained the only source of intelligence on the Russian army and navy available to the British other than intercepted German reports from the Eastern Front.

So GC&CS set up its own Russian codebreaking section at MI6 offices in Ryder Street, beginning a process that by the end of war had led to the Soviet Union becoming the main target for the codebreakers. A second GC&CS team, based in a house in Berkeley Street, had already begun deciphering messages between Moscow and its agents in the United Kingdom, providing the intelligence they produced to MI5, which had maintained an anti-Soviet section of its own throughout the war. This was based at Blenheim Palace and run by Roger Hollis, who would not only go on to be head of MI5 but was subsequently himself accused of being a Russian spy.

Despite ensuring that the Polish codebreakers continued to work on Russian codes and ciphers throughout the war and encouraging their own codebreakers to work on Russian output from the summer of 1943, it was not until October of that year that MI6 gave serious thought to human espionage operations against the Russians once the war with Germany came to an end. Valentine Vivian, MI6 Deputy Chief, proposed the creation of an anti-communist section to infiltrate foreign communist parties and gather intelligence on how they were controlled by Moscow. The Foreign Office, which had a veto on MI6 activities, agreed, with one official saying: "The Russians would simply take us for fools if we did not make use of these opportunities when it is perfectly

RIGHT Raoul Wallenberg, the Swedish diplomat who saved 100,000 Jews, was working for MI6 when he was arrested by the Russians.

clear that they have their own wide network of agents in Britain."

MI6 formally created Section IX to cover the Soviet Union in May 1944. By August it had drawn up a plan whereby MI6 officers would be sent into a post-war Soviet Union either under "official cover" as members of trade delegations or under "natural cover" as businessmen, engineers and industrialists. British spies could also be part of music, ballet, drama and sport exchanges with the Russians, one official suggested. "A start could be made now by preparing the ground with the Football Association to get them to be prepared to start work straight away." A number of companies were approached over the possibility of placing MI6 officers on their staff. These included the Hudson Bay Company, which had allowed its representative in Russia to work for MI6 in 1919; the Henry Lunn travel company; Harland and Wolff shipbuilders, who were about to start talks on the construction of icebreakers for the Russian merchant fleet; and Johnson Matthey, who were talking to Soviet officials about managing the post-war processing and sales in the West of Russian platinum and other rare metals.

The SOE was, if anything, preparing even more vigorously for the Cold War. Harold Perkins, head of the SOE's Polish Section, suggested keeping the section's operatives in Poland in place and

even sending others back to set up networks to collect intelligence and organize resistance to a Russian-controlled regime. "There are very few Englishmen who possess a first-hand knowledge of Russia, of Russian mentality and of Russian methods," Perkins added. "The Poles on the other hand have several thousand persons having those qualifications and being at the same time bitterly hostile to Russia, although friendly to us. In the event of war with Russia they would be of inestimable value to us. They represent an asset, which should not lightly be discarded." The head of SOE, Sir Colin Gubbins, ordered a list of all its agents in Central Europe to be drawn up with a view to keeping in touch with them and using them as the basis of resistance against the Russians. MI6 began attempting to infiltrate anti-communist agents into the Baltic republics and set up links with right-wing groups across Eastern Europe. Stewart Menzies, the chief of MI6, said it was essential that Britain's Soviet allies "should not become aware of the nature of the measures". Unfortunately, the man MI6 appointed to take charge of Section IX was Kim Philby, a key member of the Cambridge spy ring, who was passing details of all the British preparations for the Cold War straight back to the KGB's Moscow Centre. As a result, large numbers of British agents sent into Eastern Europe at the end of the Second World War were simply rounded up by the Russians and shot.

ABOVE The other four members of the Cambridge Five (clockwise from top left): Anthony Blunt, Donald Maclean, John Cairncross and Guy Burgess.

OPPOSITE Russian, American and British troops, still allies, stand on the balcony of Hitler's Chancellery in Berlin in July 1945.

KIM PHILBY, THE THIRD MAN

Kim Philby, who became infamous as the so-called "Third Man" in the Cambridge spy ring, was the most prominent of the Soviet agents inside British intelligence during the war. The others included John Cairncross, who worked first at Bletchley Park and then MI6; Jack Klugman, in the SOE headquarters in Cairo; and Guy Burgess, who briefly worked in Section D of MI6 and pushed for his friend Philby to be recruited as his assistant. When SOE swallowed up Section D in June 1940, Burgess was let go, but Philby became an instructor at the SOE "finishing school" at Beaulieu before being recruited into Section V of MI6 by Valentine Vivian, who knew his father. Philby had worked as a journalist covering the Spanish Civil War and was put in charge of the sub-section of Section V that covered Spain and Portugal, important countries because of their relevance to the Double Cross system. Philby was seen as the brightest of the officers brought into MI6 during the war. This and Vivian's support ensured that in 1944, when Section IX was set up to cover the emerging Soviet threat, he was the obvious man to take charge.

INDEX

PICTURE CREDITS

The publishers would like to thank the following sources for their kind permission to reproduce the pictures in this book.

Alamy: Antiqua Print Gallery 91; /APIC 151t; /John Frost Newspapers 10; /Lordprice Collection 42

Author Collection: 6t, 24, 26t, 30, 31b, 40, 41, 44, 45b, 48, 51t, 51b, 53b, 62, 89b, 93r, 108l, 116t, 122-123, 124t, 125b, 126b

Bletchley Park Trust: 15t, 15b, 16-17, 18, 19b, 95, 101l, 104

Courtesy of the NAAFI: 103

Getty Images: Walter Bellamy/Express 130t; /Bentley Archive/Popperfoto 156b; /Bettmann: 8, 94l&r, 96r, 97b, 134l; /British Official Photograph/National Archives/The LIFE Picture Collection 73b; /CBS Photo Archive 97t; /Central Press 65; /Central Press/Hulton Archive 80; /Corbis 55b; /Dennis Oulds/Central Press 20; /Dmitri Kessel 87; /Evening Standard 26 (b); / David E. Scherman/The LIFE Picture Collection 148t; /Express 68; /Galerie Bilderwelt 83b; /Tim Gidal/Hulton Archive

49; /Bernard Hoffman/The LIFE Picture Collection 66; /Hulton Archive 93l, 131r, 132l; /Hulton-Deutsch Collection/CORBIS/Corbis 128; /Kurt Hutton/Picture Post/Hulton Archive 39; /Keystone 73t, 82t, 83t, 111; /Keystone/Hulton Archive 130b, 156t; /George Konig/Keystone Features 31 (t); /LAPI/Roger Viollet 75; /Carl Mydans/The LIFE Picture Collection 96l; /Popperfoto 23t, 142-143; /SSPL 101br, 153; /136; /Reg Speller 157; /F. A. Swaine/Hulton Archive 23b

Imperial War Museums, London: 25 (H 8185), 43 (C 5663), 45t (HU 81247), 46 (CH 16106), 47 (C 3293), 102-103 (A 21715), 131 (MH 7873)

Margaret Grant Reid papers, Leeds University Library: 105, 110

The National Archives, Kew: 11-13, 27, 32-37, 50, 52, 53t, 54l&r, 55, 56-59, 61b, 63, 69-71, 76-79, 80, 84, 85, 90, 92l, 92r, 108r, 109, 113b, 115, 116b, 117, 118, 119, 125, 127t, 136l, 140, 142, 144, 146-147, 152, 155t

National Archives & Records Administration: 99, 100b, 101t

© National Portrait Gallery, London: 7tr, 83c

Norman Parkinson Archive: 22

Private Collection: 14, 19, 20r, 60t, 61t, 67, 74, 106, 107, 121, 132r

Royal Australian Air Force: 9

Science Museum/SSPL 16, 101br

Service Archives: 6b, 7l, 114, 115l

Shutterstock: George Konig 91

Topfoto.co.uk: 20c, 29, 38, 64, 82b, 88, 89b, 100t, 112, 113t, 120, 122, 129, 133, 135, 137r, 148-149, 148b, 149, 151t, 154, 155b

Every effort has been made to acknowledge correctly and contact the source and/or copyright holder of each picture and Carlton Books Limited apologises for any unintentional errors or omissions, which will be corrected in future editions of this book.